THE EMPOWERED EMPATH

A SIMPLE SURVIVAL GUIDE ON SETTING BOUNDARIES, CONTROLLING YOUR EMOTIONS, AND MAKING LIFE EASIER

BY: JUDY DYER

THE EMPOWERED EMPATH:
A Simple Guide on Setting Boundaries, Controlling Your
Emotions, and Making Life Easier
by Judy Dyer

© **Copyright 2019 by Judy Dyer**

All Rights Reserved.

ISBN-10: 1093401834
ISBN:13: 978-1093401837

ALSO BY JUDY DYER

*Empath: A Complete Guide for Developing Your Gift
and Finding Your Sense of Self*

*The Highly Sensitive: How to Stop Emotional Overload,
Relieve Anxiety, and Eliminate Negative Energy*

Empath and The Highly Sensitive: 2 in 1 Bundle

*Narcissist: A Complete Guide for Dealing with Narcissism
and Creating the Life You Want*

Empaths and Narcissists: 2 in 1 Bundle

*Borderline Personality Disorder: A Complete BPD Guide for
Managing Your Emotions and Improving Your Relationships*

CONTENTS

Introduction 7

Your Free Gift – Heyoka Empath 13

Chapter 1:   Understanding Energy 19

Chapter 2:   The Dark Side of Being an Empath 24

Chapter 3:   The Doctor Can't Help You 29

Chapter 4:   Coping Strategies: How to Cope With
             Being an Empath 32

Chapter 5:   How To Become an Assertive Empath 43

Chapter 6:   How To Control Your Emotions 48

Chapter 7:   Learning How To Set Boundaries 72

Chapter 8:   How to Become an Extroverted Empath 83

Chapter 9:   How to Block Other People's Energy 89

Chapter 10: How to Cope with a Flood of Emotions
             at One Time 95

Chapter 11: How to Find Peace Living in a Cruel World ... 101

Chapter 12: Making Career Decisions as an Empath 104

Chapter 13: How to Disconnect From What's Going
             on Around You 111

Chapter 14: How Diet Plays a Role In Energy 118

Chapter 15: Tips For Raising an Empath Child 121

Chapter 16: A Step By Step Guide To Living Your Life
             as an Empowered Empath 128

Conclusion 133

INTRODUCTION

E mpaths feel the emotions of others, from joy to pain and everything in between. They find it impossible to be in the presence of another person and not feel what they feel. Human beings want to be happy and spend the majority of their lives chasing that which they feel will complete them and bring them fulfillment. Unfortunately, most people don't find happiness—they hate their jobs, they feel trapped in unloving relationships, they feel insecure, and they want more out of life. These unfulfilled wants, needs, and desires cause sadness and depression, and people carry these feelings of heaviness every day. Unfortunately for the empath, not only do they have to deal with their own demons, but their natural ability to tune into the feelings of others forces them to deal with the demons of those they come into contact with. It is only natural to want to fight against this; after all, who wants to feel sad all the time, especially when that sadness does not belong to you?

In an attempt to stop this pain, empaths build defense mechanisms around them that prevent them from enjoying life. Despite the fortress they attempt to shield themselves with, they still absorb negative energy in the form of pain, suffering, and even illness, causing them to spend much of their lives feeling scared, sick, and lonely. Considering all that empaths are forced to endure, it is no wonder some of them are afraid to embrace their gift. However, learning how to use empathic abilities as a blessing and not a curse is essential to healthy living. Empathy is not something you can escape from—you either embrace it and use it the way it was intended or live a life of misery and suffering. You are the only person who can make that decision.

Think about a child who is naturally talented at playing the piano. When he hears music, he is able to replay it exactly as he heard it. This is his gift. He didn't learn how to play the piano, it just comes naturally to him. But if the child wants to master his craft, he is going to have to study music. If he wants to become a concert pianist, he will need to study interpersonal dynamics and practice with a group. Good teaching will accelerate his skills and enable him to become a brilliant performer or teacher. But to learn, he will need to connect with people.

In a similar fashion, empaths need to learn skills that will enhance their gift. They can shy away from this and operate on a low level, or they can enhance it and become exceptional. Empathic abilities when ignored, misused, or misunderstood can lead you into a dark place. You become weak, drained, and lifeless, burdened with responsibilities that don't belong to you, and you suffer unnecessary illness. Inasmuch as empaths have a desire to help people, taking on other people's burdens will not only hinder you but also hinder the person you are trying to help. Would you want a friend or loved one carrying your burdens? I am assuming that one hundred percent of you would answer no to this question. So, the question then becomes, if you don't want someone else carrying your burdens, why would you want to carry someone else's?

In my first book, *Empath: A Complete Guide for Developing Your Gift and Finding Your Sense of Self*, I shared with you how to recognize that you have a gift and how to tap into it; but due to popular demand, I want to answer some questions that will further help you enhance your gift and become all you were called to be.

I don't believe in coincidences. I believe in divine appointments, and you are exactly where you need to be because you are ready to step into a new level of empowerment and clarity that is going to launch you into your destiny.

In order to maximize the value you receive from this book, I highly encourage you to join our tight-knit community on Facebook. Here you will be able to connect and share with other like-minded Empaths to continue your growth.

Taking this journey alone is not recommended, and this can be an excellent support network for you.

It would be great to connect with you there,

Judy Dyer

To Join, Visit: www.pristinepublish.com/empathgroup

DOWNLOAD THE AUDIO VERSION OF THIS BOOK FREE

If you love listening to audiobooks on-the-go or would enjoy a narration as you read along, I have great news for you. You can download the audiobook version of The Empowered Empath for FREE (Regularly $14.95) just by signing up for a FREE 30-day audible trial!

Visit: www.pristinepublish.com/audiobooks

YOUR FREE GIFT - HEYOKA EMPATH

A lot of empaths feel trapped, as if they've hit a glass ceiling they can't penetrate. They know there's another level to their gift, but they can't seem to figure out what it is. They've read dozens of books, been to counselling, and confided in other experienced empaths, but that glass ceiling remains. They feel alone, and alienated from the rest of the world because they know they've got so much more to give, but can't access it. Does this sound like you?

The inability to connect to your true and authentic self is a tragedy. Being robbed of the joy of embracing the full extent of your humanity is a terrible misfortune. The driving force of human nature is to live according to one's own sense of self, values, and emotions. Since the beginning of time, philosophers, writers, and scholars have argued that authenticity is one of the most important elements of an individual's well-being.

When there's a disconnect between a person's inner being and their expressions, it can be psychologically damaging. Heyokas are the most powerful type of empaths, and many of them are not fully aware of who they are. While other empaths experience feelings of overwhelm and exhaustion from absorbing others' energy and emotions, heyoka empaths experience an additional aspect of exhaustion in that they are fighting a constant battle with their inability to be completely authentic.

The good news is that the only thing stopping you from becoming your authentic self is a lack of knowledge. You need to know exactly who you are so you can tap into the resources that have been lying dormant within you. In this bonus e-book, you'll gain in-depth information about the seven signs that you're a heyoka empath, and why certain related abilities are such powerful traits. You'll find many of the answers to the questions you've been searching for your entire life such as:

- Why you feel uncomfortable when you're around certain people
- How you always seem to find yourself on the right path even though your decisions are not based on logic or rationale
- The reason you get so offended when you find out others have lied to you
- Why you analyze everything in such detail
- The reason why humor is such an important part of your life
- Why you refuse to follow the crowd, regardless of the consequences
- The reason why strangers and animals are drawn to you

There are three main components to authenticity: understanding who you are, expressing who you are, and letting the world experience who you are. Your first step on this journey is to know who you are, and with these seven signs that you're a heyoka empath, you'll find out. I've included snippets about the first three signs in this description to give you full confidence that you're on the right track:

Sign 1: You Feel and Understand Energy

Heyoka empaths possess a natural ability to tap into energy. They can walk into a room and immediately discern the atmosphere. When an individual walks past them, they can literally see into their soul because they can sense the aura that person is carrying. But empaths also understand their own energy, and they allow it to guide them. You will often hear this ability referred to as "the sixth sense." The general consensus is that only a few people have this gift. But the reality is that everyone was born with the ability to feel energy; it's just been demonized and turned into something spooky, when in actual fact, it's the most natural state to operate in.

Sign 2: You are Led by Your Intuition

Do you find that you just know things? You don't spend hours, days, and weeks agonizing over decisions, you can just feel that something is the right thing to do, and you go ahead and do it. That's because you're led by your intuition and you're connected to the deepest part of yourself. You know your soul, you listen to it, and you trust it. People like Oprah Winfrey, Steve Jobs and Richard Branson followed their intuition steadfastly and it led them to become some of the most successful people in the history of the world.

Living from within is the way we were created to be, and those who trust this ability will find their footing in life a lot more quickly than others. Think of it as a GPS system: when it's been programmed properly, it will always take you to your destination via the fastest route.

Sign 3: You Believe in Complete Honesty

In general, empaths don't like being around negative energy, and there's nothing that can shift a positive frequency faster than dishonesty. Anything that isn't the truth is a lie, even the tiny ones that we excuse away as "white lies." And as soon as they're released from someone's mouth, so is negative energy. Living an authentic life requires complete honesty at all times, and although the truth may hurt, it's better than not being able to trust someone. Heyoka empaths get very uncomfortable in the presence of liars. They are fully aware that the vibrations of the person don't match the words they are saying. Have you ever experienced a brain freeze mid-conversation? All of a sudden you just couldn't think straight, you couldn't articulate yourself properly, and things just got really awkward? That's because your empath antenna picked up on a lie.

Heyoka Empath: 7 Signs You're A Heyoka Empath & Why It's So Powerful is a revolutionary tool that will help you transition from uncertainty to complete confidence in who you are. In this easy-to-read guide, I will walk you through exactly what makes you a heyoka empath. I've done the research for you, so no more spending hours, days, weeks, and even years searching for answers, because everything you need is right here in this book.

You have a deep need to share yourself with the world, but you've been too afraid because you knew something was missing. The information within the pages of this book is the missing piece in the jigsaw puzzle of your life. There's no turning back now!

Get *Heyoka Empath* for Free by Visiting

www.pristinepublish.com/empathbonus

CHAPTER 1:

UNDERSTANDING ENERGY

Empaths have a better understanding of energy than they do the words that are coming out of a person's mouth. This is one of the reasons you can't lie to an empath—they will sense it. Empaths can listen to someone speaking a language they don't understand but have full insight into what they are trying to express based on their energy. Empaths listen to words, pay attention to body language, and translate energetic vibrations. They are especially vulnerable to negativity because it takes from their energy field. On the other hand, when empaths are surrounded by positive energy, they become relaxed and their aura expands in an outward direction as their feelings and emotions flow freely without tension. Positive energy is like a charger—it boosts you up and refills you. This is why empaths will avoid conflict at all costs, shut down when confronted with it, and stay away from certain people and places. The body goes into self-defense mode in an attempt to preserve energy so that you don't become tired and exhausted.

Whether you know it or not, empaths can choose who and what influences their energy—they decide where it is sent and to whom. Our thoughts are so powerful that as soon as they are released, anyone capable of tuning in to your frequency will automatically pick them up. In other words, empaths have the ability to read minds. A skilled empath knows how to protect themselves by being fully aware of what is taking place around them and being present so that no one is able to enter their energy field without their permission.

Once you learn how energy works, it is important that you use it wisely. Remember what goes around comes around, and whatever you put out into the world will come right back to you. Energy is like a drug—the more you experiment with it and enjoy the way it makes you feel, the easier it is to become addicted to it. Your energy, if not protected, will abandon you, become reckless, and attach itself to any other energy circulating in the atmosphere. When empaths are alert and aware, they can quickly recognize subtle changes that take place in their environment without needing to use any of their five senses—smell, touch, taste, sight, or hearing.

Once energy has been released, it travels in an outward direction and never dies. It remains in the air and clings to people or objects, and other energies absorb it or connect with it. Our energy leaves a legacy wherever we go, which is why you can step into an environment and immediately pick up on the vibe of it. That vibe is dependent upon the people or the event that is taking place there.

Once you realize that your energy is constantly interacting with other people's energy, regardless of space, time, or distance, it can become overwhelming, and you will feel as though you need to get back to yourself. But this is because society has conditioned us to believe that our mind and body are two separate entities.

Empaths have a deep desire to discover who they are and what they were put on this earth to do. The awakening process is an extremely traumatic and painful one, parallel to the metamorphosis of the caterpillar into a butterfly. It is a dark and lonely time, but once you discover your truth, you will emerge like a beautiful butterfly and soar to new heights. It is during this time that you come to the revelation that we are not separate or individual but a part of something tremendous—energy and the universe.

You are not always going to be able to explain your gift because there are some aspects of it that are illogical, and in a world that relies on logic, mathematics, and scientific studies, this can be difficult to comprehend. Empaths feel and sense their way through life. They do not need men in white coats to explain what they inherently know about their natural existence. People who don't understand the gift will chalk it up to whatever their imaginations can conjure up and refuse to believe that such a thing exists. Such people are afraid to challenge the status quo and think outside the box; they are afraid of the unknown. They are confined by what they can see with their natural eyes, and if they can't see it, they won't believe it.

Once you have extensive knowledge of how energy works, you will immediately discover limitless mind-blowing possibilities. You will realize that your energy never dies and in whatever form it takes, it will continue to exist.

When your life is determined by time, you can become disillusioned, especially if you have reached a certain age and not achieved all that you had hoped. When you were 16, you had envisioned that you would be married with kids by the age of 30. But by the age of 35, you still haven't found your soul mate and so you start worrying about how much time you have left to fulfill your dreams. You realize that you have wasted your time slaving away in a job that you don't like, or that you have married the wrong person and allowed your soulmate to slip through your fingers.

In reality, time doesn't exist. The universe has no regard for it. Man created time, and we have structured our lives around it. If time was abolished, there would be mayhem because people wouldn't know what to do with themselves. When we get to a certain age and our bodies start to decay, we assume that time is running out. But even when our bodies have returned to dust, our energy will continue to travel throughout the universe—there is no beginning and no end. We existed before we took residence on earth in a human body, and we will continue to exist when this body disintegrates.

Physically and mentally, empaths are different. Our bodies are porous, so they absorb energy into their muscles, organs, and tissues. This means that you feel other people's pain, distress, suffering, and depression. You can feel every negative emotion even though they don't belong to you, which can have a detrimental effect on your health. On the other hand, you can quickly get in tune with other people's love, happiness, and vitality, which is a fantastic feeling.

Empaths feel exhausted when they are surrounded by toxic people, witnessing arguments, violence, and hearing too much noise makes empaths feel physically ill.

Empaths can also feel other people's physical pain and pick up the same symptoms as if they had the illness. This is one of the reasons they find it difficult to work in hospitals. You might find that your mood changes when you get on a bus and sit next to someone who is depressed or anxious. Or you can walk into a store feeling happy or even neutral, but leave feeling tense and exhausted, or even with aches and pains in your body because you have been exposed to the whirlwind of chaos that usually takes place in a store with the bright lights, loud speakers, and crowds of people. There are certain environments that are simply not conducive for empaths.

To survive as an empath, it's crucial to learn how to ground yourself in overstimulating situations and protect yourself against other people's negative energy.

CHAPTER 2:

THE DARK SIDE OF BEING AN EMPATH

There is no doubt that empaths have been blessed with a unique gift; but unfortunately, it can become a curse if you don't understand it and know how to control it. As I am sure you are aware, constantly feeling the stress and pain of others can leave you feeling drained and lifeless. Since your neurological and biological makeup absorbs the emotions of others on a large scale, a lot of empaths experience serious health problems including:

- Headaches
- Back pain
- Digestive issues
- Anxiety
- Chronic depression
- A weak immune system
- Chronic fatigue

On a social level, empaths are extremely compassionate. This trustworthy trait is very appealing to people who are suffering. Unfortunately, many empaths are taken advantage of because of this, and they tend to attract the worst kinds of people—sociopaths, narcissists, and people with a general manipulative character. It has been argued that one of the reasons sociopaths are attracted to empaths is because they don't have any emotions, and so they look to others to fill that void. Empaths are highly emotional people, and sociopaths instinctively know this. They lure the empath in through eye contact, subtle gestures, mannerisms, and body language. Empaths are drawn to this because of their attraction to special feelings.

Empaths find it difficult to make personal choices because they pay so much attention to the emotions of others. They are always worrying about how their decisions might affect the people around them. This leads them to create an image of perfectionism, and there is always a conflict between pleasing others and pleasing themselves. Some empaths want people to think they are perfect, hence their desire to please others, which is a constant struggle (you will learn more about this in chapter 6).

Empaths are very in tune with their instincts, which makes it easy for them to read people immediately. However, being aware of other people's difficulties can become problematic. There is often an overlap between their feelings and the feelings of others, which can have a negative effect on the confidence of an empath. Empaths often find it difficult to understand why they feel the way they do. They often ask themselves, "Am I personally experiencing anxiety or is it coming from someone else?" Some empaths don't know how to handle the emotional overload and will turn to drugs and alcohol as a coping mechanism.

Empaths are often mistaken as being overly sensitive and weak, which can have a negative effect on their self-esteem. Additionally, they find it difficult to watch violent or graphic content and will avoid watching the news or TV in general. They also feel uncomfortable discussing misfortune, cruelties, and injustices.

CHALLENGES FOR EMPATH MALES AND FEMALES

Male and female empaths experience some of the same, but also different challenges. Empaths are sensitive people—females can show this side of them openly, but males find it difficult because of the social stigma attached to overly emotional men. Boys are raised not to cry, to be strong and macho, and displaying their sensitivities is seen as a sign of weakness. Boys with such characteristics are often bullied at school and labeled as "sissies" and "cry babies." Therefore, empath males find it difficult to talk about how they feel in fear of being judged as not masculine enough. They are not interested in sports like basketball, baseball, and soccer; neither are they interested in aggressive contact sports such as rugby and wrestling, and so they may feel isolated and rejected by their peers. As a result, male empaths tend to repress their emotions and act as if they don't exist. They often suffer in silence feeling that no one understands them, which can have a negative impact on their health, relationships, and careers.

Alanis Morrissette, a known empath, wrote a song entitled "In Praise of the Vulnerable Man." Men must embrace their sensitive nature because it is nothing to be ashamed of. This does not mean being overly feminine, it means being balanced, owning both your masculine and feminine sides. It means being secure enough to be vulnerable and strong enough to be sensitive. Men of this nature have high emotional intelligence. They do not fear their own or other people's emotions, which makes them attractive and compassionate partners, leaders, and friends.

Females, on the other hand, don't experience the same challenges when it comes to emotional sensitivity. Girls are raised to express their emotions—it's okay for them to cry and feel sad. The notion of female intuition is also socially acceptable, but the idea of females being powerful is still frowned upon in Western society. Historically, women have had to and are still fighting for equality. Females have experienced horrendous struggles because of their gender. More than 200 women were arrested and approximately 20 were slaughtered during the Salem witch trials because of their sensitivities.

Even though it is somewhat acceptable, women today are still afraid to express their sensitivities in fear of being judged or misunderstood. This is especially true in relationships because overly emotional women are often deemed as being needy and insecure. It's important that female empaths learn to be authentic in their relationships and openly discuss their needs. They should know how to set boundaries with their time and energy so they don't get overwhelmed and experience burn out. Male or female, an empath who knows how to give and receive in a balanced way holds a lot of power.

CHAPTER 3:

THE DOCTOR CAN'T HELP YOU

Empaths who don't understand their gift will go and see a health care practitioner for help. They are often misdiagnosed as neurotics, hypochondriacs, or in need of psychiatric assistance for depression or anxiety and prescribed with medication such as Xanax, Valium, or Prozac. This is not what someone dealing with empathetic overload needs. Empaths are also misdiagnosed with Sensory Processing Disorder in which sufferers have difficulty processing sensory stimulation. People with the disorder are said to have an abnormal sensitivity to touch, sound, light, and crowds. Traditional medicine tends to pathologize anything that it doesn't understand.

Unlike alternative medicine, conventional medicine is ignorant about how the human body and energy work together. The body has a distinct energy field, and empaths are extremely sensitive to this. If mainstream medicine is to be of any benefit to highly sensitive people, it needs to gain a thorough understanding of this.

You cannot cure empathy. It is not a medical condition, so prescribing empaths with anti-depressants and anti-anxiety medication is of no use. Empaths simply need to make certain adjustments to their lives, which is what you will learn how to do in the pages of this book. Sometimes, the adjustment is a simple one, and sometimes it is not so simple. For example, Alice went to see her physician because she found it too stressful and experienced severe anxiety when getting on the underground to go to work. Although Alice practiced meditation and other exercises before traveling, it did not relieve her feelings of distress, and so she was prescribed with anti-anxiety medication. She knew she didn't suffer from anxiety because she didn't feel like this all the time, so Alice didn't take the medication and looked for alternative treatment. Her search led her to Juliet, a psychiatrist that happens to be an empath, who suggested that she drive to work instead and avoid rush hour traffic by waking up earlier. Alice was extremely happy with this solution and wondered why she hadn't thought of it herself. She was also reminded that she is a unique individual with unique needs, and she shouldn't feel guilty about being different, which is something that empaths have trouble accepting. You are not like everyone else, and you should stop trying to be. A part of embracing your gift is accepting the fact that you are special. If people can't understand it, that's their problem and not yours. There is no failure in finding ways to cope and deal with your needs, but turning to medication is not one of them.

Now, please note, if you are an empath who has experienced abuse, trauma, or any other type of tragedy, you are going to need psychological help, so please get it. It is also important to mention that due to the highly sensitive nature of an empath when it comes to psychotropic medication, you typically require a lower dosage than everyone else. So, if you do need to take medication, I suggest that you visit an integrative healthcare practitioner who understands subtle energy and will work with you to find the dose that will benefit you the most.

CHAPTER 4:

COPING STRATEGIES: HOW TO COPE WITH BEING AN EMPATH

L iving as an empath is difficult. No one understands your gift, and you feel constantly drained because everyone is pulling on your energy, and the truth is that sometimes you feel as if you are living in a nightmare! The thing is, as I am sure you are well aware, you can't take the gift back to the shop to get a refund—it's yours for life. You can't turn your back on being an empath. It's not the same as a singing gift or an athletic gift where you can just decide that you are not going to sing or play basketball anymore. You have to learn to live a happy and productive life as an empath. So here are some unique coping strategies to help you do this.

EMBRACE YOUR CREATIVE SIDE

Empaths are generally very creative people. They like to draw, paint, and dance, all of which can be very therapeutic. You have a desire to want to save the world from its many troubles, and while this is an admirable goal, the truth is that it's impossible. Expressing yourself through your creativity is a great way to eliminate negative energy and create something beautiful that you can control and be proud of. It is also a way of purging some of the frustration that comes from not being able to heal the planet.

Find something that you are good at, and practice it daily. Incorporate your creativity into your daily routine and you will start to feel less stressed and frustrated about being an empath.

INDEPENDENT LIVING

One of the things that empaths dislike about their gift is that it makes them feel cluttered. They pick up emotions and energy from everywhere, and they want to escape from it all. You are constantly bombarded with stress and negativity, whether it's from people or through the media, and your one desire is to get away.

Empaths find it difficult to separate their true identity from the emotions of others. You are very idealistic and are constantly thinking of ways to improve the lives of others. This strong desire to help people can become compulsive. If you are not an empath and are reading this, you now understand why your friend is so obsessive when it comes to finding solutions to your problems. When listening to a problem, empaths will often come up with an immediate solution and do everything in their power to help fix it. Although this is a good quality to have, it can lead empaths to become emotionally co-dependent because you are constantly relying on the happiness of others to feel satisfied.

The assumption is that there is only one type of co-dependency, which is where a person is emotionally or financially reliant upon an individual to take care of them. Another form of co-dependency is when a person's satisfaction in life is derived from their ability to please and help other people. This is the type of co-dependency that empaths often suffer from. If you read any books about co-dependency, you will find the characteristics of an unskilled empath described on every page, including:

- Feeling guilt, pity, and anxiety when other people are experiencing problems
- The belief that you are responsible for the choices, well-being, needs, wants, actions, and feelings of others
- Wondering why they don't receive the same treatment from others
- Not knowing how or when to verbalize their wants and needs because they don't know what they are and they don't view them as important as everyone else's
- Doing things for other people that they don't want to do and then getting angry about it
- Feeling compelled to help people whether they ask for it or not and refusing to accept help from others because they feel guilty
- Feeling sad because they pour so much into others, but they don't receive the same back from others
- Feeling empty or useless when they don't have a problem or crisis to resolve or someone to help

- Needy people are always attracted to them
- Putting others' needs before their own
- Feeling used, unappreciated, victimized, and angry

These co-dependent characteristics describe the unskilled empath because empaths have an innate inclination to want to make things better; they are natural healers. But putting so much energy into restoring and pleasing other people is emotionally draining. Empaths need to cut themselves off from this behavior and understand that happiness comes from within and nowhere else.

For example, Mike comes home from work after a bad day, and instead of greeting his wife, he stomps up the stairs, goes into his room, and slams the door. Susan, his wife, is an empath, and she automatically detects that there is something wrong because she starts to feel his pain. She does everything she can think of to make him feel better, but nothing works. Every day, he comes home in the same bad mood. Susan spends her days looking for solutions to a problem she doesn't understand, and her evenings trying to implement them. Her life is centered around her husband and improving his mood. This is what co-dependence is like for an empath. Susan can break her back trying to rectify her husband's problem, but if he is unwilling to talk about it and it is due to a stressful situation at work, until he decides to open up or do something about it himself, there is nothing she can do to help him. The real solution is that Susan must learn to live independently from her husband's problems.

Have you been through a similar experience? Maybe the emotions of others are making it difficult for you to get things done. When you run into situations like this, you need to evaluate the problem to see where it is coming from because, like the example with Mike and Susan, there are going to be times when there is nothing you can do to actively resolve the situation. Your only option will be to offer your support and give your friend or partner the space to deal with their issues. Since you are an energy sponge, you should keep your distance from that person until they have gotten over the crisis. You can still support them without compromising your emotional wellbeing.

DAILY YOGA

Yoga is a powerful method to help get rid of unwanted energy. The combination of postures, deep breathing, and relaxation are essential to releasing tension and blocked energy. To release yourself from holding onto pain, whether it's yours or someone else's, you must let your life force travel freely within your body. So here are a few tips to get you started. You can also buy books, DVDs, or join a yoga class.

BASIC BREATHING TECHNIQUE

- Sit on the ground, cross your legs, straighten your back, and place your hands over your knees.
- Close your eyes and take a deep breath in through your nose—your stomach should rise when you do this.

- Hold your breath for four seconds.
- Breathe out for four seconds—your stomach should deflate when you do this.
- Repeat this for five minutes.

YOGA POSES TO RELEASE NEGATIVE EMOTIONS

Here are three yoga poses to help you release negative energy and allow positive energy to flow freely throughout your body.

1. **Facing Upwards Dog**

    To get rid of unwanted emotions, effective communication is essential. This yoga position helps to relieve tension in the throat and unblock and balance the throat chakra.

    - Lay a mat down on the floor.
    - Lie on your stomach, extend your legs behind you, and push the front of your feet into the ground.
    - Position your hands flat on the mat directly underneath your shoulders.
    - Inhale and use your hands to push your upper body up off the ground.
    - Once you are in an upwards position, exhale.
    - Stay like this for 10 seconds at the same time inhaling and exhaling.

2. **Angle Bound Pose**

    Much of our emotional energy and trauma is held in our hips. The angle bound pose will loosen up your hips and help move stuck energy throughout the body.

- Sit in a crossed leg position on your mat but allow the soles of your feet to touch.
- Place your hands over your feet and split them apart as if you are opening a book.
- Take a deep breath in and stretch your spine upwards.
- Exhale and relax your knees allowing them to fall towards the ground.
- Repeat this for 10 breaths.

3. **The Plank Pose**

The plank pose helps to strengthen your core, and it is good for the central nervous system. When our bodies feel strong, we also feel strong emotionally and mentally, which allows you to cope with any challenges that may come your way.

- Lie on your stomach with your palms on the floor directly under your shoulders.
- Your legs should be extended behind you (shoulder width apart) with the balls of your toes pressing into the ground.
- Inhale and push your entire body off the ground using your hands and feet.
- Remain in this position for 10 seconds at the same time inhaling and exhaling.

TURN YOUR HOME INTO A PROTECTIVE HAVEN

You should feel safe in your personal space; it is important that you create an environment that you are totally comfortable in. The mood and atmosphere of your home should reflect the way you feel inside. If you are not happy with your living quarters, you are going to have to make some changes.

What does your wardrobe look like? Your drawers? Underneath your bed? Are things just stuffed and piled up all over the place? As you have read, energy travels and attaches itself to objects, people, and other energy. When you are in an environment with a lot of negative people, you start feeling exhausted, hopeless, depleted, and distressed. When you are in an environment with positive people, you feel a sense of calm; you feel healthy and in control of your energy. Now let's take a look at how an untidy and tidy home can make you feel.

A Cluttered and Dirty Home…

Makes you feel exhausted. An untidy home is similar to an energy vampire. Negative energy attaches itself to objects, and simply being in such an environment will drain you.

Makes you feel hopeless. A never-ending pile of mess is psychologically overwhelming. You feel as if you will never get through it all so there is no point in even trying to clean it.

A Tidy and Organized Home...

Makes you feel calm. You can relax and unwind in a tidy home. There is space to do things, and you know where everything is. When you walk into a hotel room, you immediately feel a sense of peace because the environment is tidy and organized.

Makes you feel healthy. Dust and mold accumulate in messes. Are you always coughing and sneezing? Do you suffer from allergies? It's probably because you are breathing in all the dirt in your home. Give your home a spring clean and your health issues will improve.

Makes you feel in control. How does it feel when you know where everything is? Clutter prevents positive energy from flowing through your home. Remember, energy attaches itself to objects, and negative energy is attracted to mess, which creates exhaustion, stagnation, and exasperation. What does it feel like when negative energy is stuck in your body? You want to lie in bed and shut the world away because everything becomes more difficult and you can't explain why.

Here is how decluttering your house will unlock blocked streams of positive energy:

You will become more vibrant. Once you create harmony and order in your home, you will feel more radiant and present. Like acupuncture, which removes imbalances and blockages from the body to create more wellness and dynamism, clearing clutter removes imbalances and blockages from your personal space. When you venture through spaces that have been set ablaze with fresh energy, you are captured by inspiration, and the most attractive parts of your personality come to life.

You will get rid of bad habits and introduce good ones. All bad habits have triggers. Do you lie on your bed to watch TV instead of sitting on the couch because you can't be bothered to fold the laundry that has piled up over the past six months? Or because the bed represents sleep, and when you come home from work and get into bed, you are going to fall asleep instead of doing those important tasks on your to-do list. Once you tidy the couch, coming home from work will allow you to sit on it to watch your favorite TV program but get up once it's finished and do what you need to do.

You will improve your problem-solving skills. When your home has been opened up with a clear space, it's easier to focus, which provides you with a fresh perspective on your problems.

You will sleep better. Are you always tired no matter how much sleep you get? That's because negative energy is stuck under your bed amongst all that junk you've stuffed under there. Once you tidy up your bedroom, you will find that positive energy can flow freely around your room making it easier for you to have a deep and restful sleep.

You will have more time. Mess delays you. An untidy house means you are always losing things. You can't find a shoe, a sock, or your keys, so you waste time searching for them, which makes you late for work or social gatherings. When you declutter your home, you could save about an hour a day because you will no longer need to dig through a stack of items to find things.

Your intuition will be stronger. A clear space creates a sense of certainty and clarity. You know where everything is, so you have peace of mind. When you have peace of mind, you can focus on being in the present moment. When you need to make important decisions, you will find it easier to do so.

It might take some time to give your home a deep clean, but you won't be sorry for it once it's done.

CHAPTER 5:

HOW TO BECOME AN ASSERTIVE EMPATH

T he word assertive means *"having or showing a confident and forceful personality."* Assertiveness is a powerful quality to have, and even more so if you are an empath. Empaths can be so kind that they neglect themselves. Highly sensitive people understand the negative effect that conflict has on their energy. Just being present when there is a disagreement or an argument can cause them severe distress. Therefore, empaths stay away from any type of conflict even when their beliefs are challenged. This is one of the reasons empaths are targeted by manipulators—they would rather agree with you than get into an argument. This is why assertiveness should be a part of your character. It will ensure that you don't allow others to walk all over you and that you are capable of standing up for yourself when necessary.

STAND UP FOR YOURSELF

The average person doesn't understand empaths; in fact, most people have never heard of the term and have a tendency to label highly sensitive people as mentally challenged. This type of judgment can lead empaths to feel ashamed of their gift, keep quiet about it, and try and act as if it doesn't exist. In reality, a lot of people wish they had the ability to tune into the emotions of others; it would make life a whole lot easier, especially in romantic and work relationships. Imagine being able to detect when your significant other is feeling down, even though they haven't said anything? Or knowing when not to send your manager that email about a pay raise because they are not in the best of moods?

Empaths shouldn't be ashamed of their ability. They should embrace their gift and be proud of it. Don't allow others to look down on you for the sake of avoiding conflict. I am not saying you should get involved in full blown arguments about your abilities, but spend time educating yourself about your gift, so that you feel more confident when explaining it to others. Another aspect of being assertive is that you know who you are, you are confident in your own skin, and you are not going to conform to anyone else's standards but your own.

Repressing your emotions can have a negative effect on your psyche, and this is something that empaths do to avoid conflict. They get into situations where they should have verbalized their disagreement of something but failed to do so in case an argument broke out. One way to get over your fear of defending yourself is to change your definition of conflict. It is natural to disagree with people. We are unique beings with different opinions, ideas, and perspectives, so we are bound to challenge each other every once in a while. Instead of seeing conflict as something negative, look at it as a normal part of life. People stand up for their rights and for what they believe in every day. In fact, you will gain more respect if you speak up for yourself. Even if the other person in the conversation is getting aggressive, you can respond in a calm but assertive manner. No matter how you feel, refrain from showing signs of irritation, anger, or fear, you don't want to give the impression that what the other person said has had a negative effect on you.

LET OTHERS KNOW WHAT YOU NEED

Because empaths are so compassionate and have a tendency to want to please and help others, people feel comfortable confiding in them. Are you always providing a listening ear to your friends, associates, and family members when they have a problem? Does this type of interaction leave you feeling emotionally drained and unable to focus on your daily tasks? Because you always provide the shoulder to cry on, do you find it difficult to let those closest to you know when you are hurting?

Letting people know what you need will have a positive effect on your energy field. You are going to feel uncomfortable when you first start doing this because it is not something that you are used to doing. But once you realize how much better it makes you feel, it will become easier for you. There are going to be times when your needs inconvenience someone else; there is nothing wrong with this— let the shoe be on the other foot for a change. Empaths are always going out of their way to help others, now it's your turn. You should also think about your needs and how they relate to your health, and constantly allowing people to drain your energy is going to leave you feeling exhausted, tired, and in the worst case, sick. There is nothing selfish about thinking like this, as these are steps you are going to have to take if you want to maintain balance in your life.

Your friends and loved ones should care about your health needs. Tell them what it's like being an empath because they probably don't know. Most people are just going to assume that you are an extremely loving and kind person. Let them know your triggers, and the environments and atmospheres you feel uncomfortable in. You should also explain to them how important it is for you to have space. If necessary, block off a day and time during the week and request that no one contact you. When those around you know what you need, they are more likely to respect your wishes.

Empaths often feel uncomfortable letting their friends and family members know when they have a problem because they are always the ones lending a supporting ear. Some empaths even feel guilty when they express negative emotions, which leads you to keep things to yourself and repress your feelings. This is a dangerous way to live because repressed emotions can cause medical conditions such as heart disease and arthritis. You are just as important as anyone else in the world, and you deserve the same time and attention as the next person. A conversation with someone who cares about how you feel will help to recharge your batteries.

You are an extraordinary individual with your own set of aspirations and goals. People are not always going to understand your passions, and the truth is that they don't need to. When it comes to decision making, the people around you are going to have a difficult time understanding your natural intuitive ability to know whether something is right or wrong. This can scare people and cause them to want to make decisions for you in fear that you are making the wrong one. One of the gifts you hold as an empath is the ability to feel when something is wrong or right. Be careful not to allow others to think for you—listen to your inner voice and follow it. When friends and family members attempt to intervene in your decision-making process, let them know in no uncertain terms that your mind is made up and you are not going to change it. Once people start to see that you are capable of making the right decisions, they will begin to respect you and your decisions, and this will increase your confidence.

CHAPTER 6:

HOW TO CONTROL YOUR EMOTIONS

Living as an empath is like being on a constant emotional roller coaster. One minute you are fine, and the next your head is spinning in a whirlwind of thoughts and feelings, and you are not quite sure where they came from. The good news is that it is possible to control your emotions. You don't need to live in a state of constant turmoil. Here are a few tips to assist you.

DON'T EXPECT EVERYONE TO LIVE UP TO YOUR EXPECTATIONS

As an empath, you've got strong feelings. You can tune in to what people are thinking by reading their reaction, and this can sometimes send your mind into overdrive. Have you ever spent time talking to someone only to find that you can't get the conversation out of your head after you get home? You spend every waking moment going over the details of the discussion and you end up drawing conclusions about how the person feels about you. Nine times out of ten, your brain will trick you into believing that they don't really like you, or that they didn't really agree with what you were saying. You might also feel disappointed that the person you were speaking to didn't feel the same level of compassion as you. But you have to remember that first, you are a highly sensitive person, so things are going to affect you more than they are going to affect others. And second, people are always going to have different opinions—what overwhelms your heart may not overwhelm somebody else's.

We live in a fallen world, nothing is perfect here and it never will be. Ideally, everyone should be kind and loving to one another, but as you know, that's simply not the case. The reality is that there are wicked, narcissistic, and evil people walking the earth who can take a life without thinking twice about it. You only have to turn on the TV or open a newspaper to see how much evil takes place in the world every day. It would be magnificent for you if everyone was an empath, if everyone had the emotional capacity to shoulder the burdens of others, but this is simply not the case. You have no power over the way other people think, and there is no point in wasting your energy trying to change it. When you come to the conclusion that in general people are not going to share the same level of compassion as you, it will make your life a lot easier because you won't spend so much time living in disappointment. You will be able to brush things off and keep moving.

Not everyone is going to agree with you. In fact, some of your friends and family are going to make decisions that are in direct conflict with yours. You will decide to go one way, and they will decide to go another, and there is absolutely nothing wrong with this. When it happens (because it will), let it go. Everyone is entitled to their own opinions and has their own life decisions to make, whether you agree with them or not. You might feel in your spirit that a friend is making the wrong choice, so unless they ask you to intervene, leave them to it. Some people will have to learn the hard way and consequence is the best teacher. When you try to convince others to do something that is against their will, you waste a lot of energy. Situations like this leave you feeling drained and exhausted.

Not forcing your expectations on others is one of the most important life lessons I have learned. There is nothing more time consuming than trying to get others to see things from your point of view. It's a waste of time, parallel to speaking Chinese to a man who only speaks English— they will never understand! And that's ok. When it comes to your expectations, the only person you should be concerned about living up to them is you.

HAVE YOUR TOOL KIT WITH YOU AT ALL TIMES

There are plenty of tools available for empaths to use in everyday situations. To make life easier for yourself, you should have them ready and available to use at all times. If you are sensitive to temperature, light, or sound and you know you have to leave the house, make sure you take what you need with you. If you drive, I would advise that you keep a spare set of these items in the car, so you don't have to worry about packing them every time you leave the house.

If you are sensitive to loud noise, carry noise-canceling headphones. If you don't have a pair already, you can buy small discreet earbuds that you can wear in any environment. Carry a sweater, cardigan, or t-shirt in case the temperature changes. Empaths can find it distressing when they are too hot or too cold.

Preparation is your best defense against protecting your energy. You will experience less anxiety when you know that you have everything you need just in case of an emergency.

SET LIMITS WITH TECHNOLOGY USE

Empaths may love technology more than anyone else. Since they like to isolate themselves, it allows them to communicate without being present in social situations. But it also has its downsides. When you are constantly available online, it gives energy vampires easy access to you, and that is definitely something you want to avoid. Also, people can post the most distressing and heartbreaking news on social media. In recent years, several violent deaths and suicides have been posted online. Sometimes, energy vampires are not people, but the platforms that you are constantly scrolling. Do you ever feel drained after looking through your Instagram or Facebook feed? It is possible for you to absorb negative energy when you spend too much time online.

Setting limits or abstaining from social media for a period of time can promote mental clarity and restore energy levels. Set yourself a technology time limit of 30 minutes to one hour per day. This is just enough time to do what you need to do without getting sucked into all the drama that takes place online.

HOW TO RESTORE YOUR ENERGY

One of the negative effects of being an empath is a constant loss of energy. You can avoid this when you need to. But a natural part of being an empath is opening your energy fields for the greater good, which will leave you feeling drained. The good news is that there are techniques you can incorporate into your life to restore your energy levels. The healing process no longer solely involves medicine and therapy; people seeking help now have a range of options to choose from. Here are a few practical techniques that can assist you in maintaining balance and restoring your energy levels.

Acupuncture: Empaths often suffer from digestive issues and lower back pain because of the negative energy they carry in these areas. Acupuncture is an ancient Chinese treatment, and one of the many ways in which it works is through balancing vital energy. It involves inserting needles into certain parts of the body to promote the free flow of energy. Acupuncture improves the circulation of oxygen and blood throughout the body, which promotes energy production at the cellular level. Additionally, acupuncture improves the digestive function, which is vital to providing essential nutrients that support energy production to the body.

You may have heard of the term "chi." Ancient Chinese practitioners use it to refer to a person's energy or balance. Acupuncture treatment is deeply relaxing. It brings the body's system back into alignment creating a healthy balance that enables energy levels to recover and rebuild themselves.

Your mantra: Empaths possess the unique ability to read people with precision and accuracy. However, they find it difficult to understand their own emotions. Mantras are short powerful statements that remind you of your life's direction. They are more than inspirational quotes that provoke people to take action. They are powerful words that call what you want into your reality. Some empaths will not engage in social activities or spend time with people unless they have repeated their mantra. Here are some powerful mantras that you might want to consider using:

- I control where my energy goes, and I will not allow others to take it from me.
- I have the confidence to express what I need and defend myself when necessary.
- I will disassociate myself from toxic situations without feeling ashamed.

Once you have chosen your mantra(s), get into the habit of saying them every day. You might feel a bit strange saying them at first because, in reality, you don't actually believe the words that are coming out of your mouth. But the more you say them, the more you will start to believe them, and they will eventually become a part of your core belief system.

I love mantras because you have full control over what you say. Spend some time defining your own mantras. You will be surprised at how much fun you have with them.

Palliative care: Palliative care is also known as "supportive care." It is treatment, support, and care for terminally ill patients. The aim is to improve quality of life by being as active and healthy as possible in the time they have left. It can involve:

- Managing painful physical symptoms
- Psychological, spiritual, and emotional support
- Support for family and friends
- Help with things such as eating, dressing, and washing

Ok, so you are probably thinking that being an empath is not a terminal illness, so how is palliative care going to help me? Well, another aspect of palliative care is palliative arts, which involves engaging in purposeful activity to add meaning and enrich life. This type of therapy involves patients dealing with their emotions through activities such as sculpting, painting, writing poetry, and listening to music. This enables them to focus on their negative emotions by expressing them in a positive light. Since empaths are typically creative people, this is a great way to relieve some of the tension associated with being a highly sensitive person. Empaths also find it difficult to express negative emotions to others, so this is another way of releasing energy that does not benefit you without the fear of being judged.

Change your thought process: Your thoughts dictate your actions, so if you want to change the way you react to certain situations, you are going to have to change the way you think. This is easier said than done because our thought patterns stem from years of social conditioning. When people or situations are overstimulating, it is easy to ignore it or justify it by accepting that this is "just the way things are," when in reality, you should have taken some type of action. There are also going to be times when you are so used to helping other people that compassion has become your crutch. For example, a friend of yours is in an abusive relationship. Every other week she is calling you crying about the latest fight she just had with her boyfriend. You keep telling her to get out of the relationship, but she keeps going back. You keep answering the phone even though speaking to her is draining because you feel her pain and want to help her to overcome it. But the reality of the situation is that there is nothing you can practically do to help her; she has to make her own decisions.

By changing the way you think about things, you change your reality. The way you look at situations and your tolerance levels will also change. No longer will you allow people to treat you as a dumping ground for their problems. The bottom line is that your mind is not a trash can, and when people are constantly offloading their issues onto you that's what they are indirectly saying. Remember, garbage in, garbage out. Whatever you allow into your system consistently is what is going to come out. One of the main reasons empaths always feel depleted is because they let too many people dump their rubbish onto them. You will start recognizing your own self-destructive behavioral patterns and adjust them before they start to have a negative effect on your life.

How do I Change the Way I Think?

Changing the way you think is not an easy process—it takes time and practice. In the field of psychology, this is referred to as cognitive behavioral therapy (CBT). The treatment takes a hands-on and practical approach to problem-solving. The end goal is to change the behavior and thinking patterns that contribute to the issues that people are dealing with. It is used to treat a range of psychological illnesses such as anxiety, depression, insomnia, and addiction. CBT works by changing a person's attitudes and behavior by focusing on the thoughts and beliefs that are held by the patient. This is called "cognitive processes," and they are evaluated to discover how a person handles emotional problems.

You don't need to see a therapist to practice cognitive behavioral therapy. You can if you wish, but there are plenty of books that will walk you through the process. In the meantime, here are some steps that you can put into practice immediately.

RECOGNIZE YOUR THOUGHT PATTERNS

Negative thinking leads to stress, fear, anxiety, and a whole host of unwanted emotions. Once you learn to identify the negative thought patterns as they happen, you can step back from them. This process is called "cognitive defusion," where you learn to see the thoughts in your head as thoughts and not reality. The problem is that we don't realize how powerful our thoughts are. We can become so attached to them that they play out in our everyday lives. When we can step outside of ourselves and look at our thoughts for what they really are, and only listen to them if they add value to our lives, things will start to change for the better.

The first thing I want you to know is that there is nothing wrong with having negative thoughts. I know that sounds like an absolute contradiction to everything you have just read but hear me out. If you look back into human history when we were hunters and gatherers, the mind was programmed to look out for dangers and problems. Our ancestors didn't live in houses where they could keep the door locked at night, so they had to protect themselves against wild animals, which meant that they were constantly thinking about new protection strategies. Now, there is nothing positive about thinking a 10-foot bear is going to come and eat you and your children in the middle of the night is there? But, unfortunately, that was their reality. They had to think like that to outsmart the wild animals. Today's problems are much different. We no longer need to worry about predators attacking our families in the middle of the night, but we still need to think about protection strategies.

For example, a husband and wife have to think about what would happen if one of them were to get sick or die. This is why people get insurance—to make sure they are covered if the worst does happen. There is nothing positive about anticipating death, but it is a reality everyone has to think about, and if you don't, you will end up stuck in a rut when something does happen.

The problem isn't the thought, the problem is believing that these thoughts are true. So, for example, back to your friend who won't leave her bad relationship. You lie awake at night thinking about it. Your main concern is that if she doesn't leave him, she could get seriously hurt or worst-case scenario, he might kill her. There is nothing wrong with thinking like this because it is normal to worry about your friend. The problem is that you feel that you have to cater to her every need any time she calls. Your thought process is if you don't answer the phone, she won't think you are a good friend, or that she won't be able to cope without you. You are so attached to your thoughts that you believe them wholeheartedly, and so you pick up the phone every time she calls and allow her to dump her trash on you.

The reality is that you don't know what your friend is thinking and neither do you know if she will be able to cope if you don't continue to baby her. So, because you don't know this as a fact, they are simply thoughts that you can allow to pass by without focusing on them. Now that you have come to this conclusion, you are free to lie in bed at night and think about something that edifies you instead.

Most people have become so used to negative thinking

that it has become a habit. They don't even know when they are doing it, so you have to train yourself to recognize unhelpful thinking patterns. Here are some of the most common, how to recognize them, and what you can do to stop them from dominating your mind.

NEGATIVE SELF TALK AND CRITICISM

It is often said that we are our own worst enemy—this is a very true statement. You may think that you spend the majority of your time talking to your significant other, but the truth is that the majority of your time is spent speaking to yourself! I thought this was the most ridiculous statement I had ever heard when it was first introduced to me, but the more I analyzed it, the more it made sense. You see, each one of us has an inner voice, and depending on how we tune in, it can be either positive or negative.

Negative self-talk and criticism is when you are constantly berating yourself. You highlight all your flaws and tell yourself that you are not good enough, and neither will you ever be good enough. You beat yourself up because you haven't reached your idea of perfection. Empaths probably suffer from this more than most, especially when they can't fix other people. They feel as if it's their fault and that the reason the other person is failing is because they can't come up with the right solution to their problems. This leads to feelings of low self-worth and low self-esteem.

There is nothing wrong with wanting to help people, but you have to realize that first, you can't help everyone, and second, no matter what you do, some people will only change when they decide to. When the mind is continuously focused on what you are not capable of, you will invite more of these things into your life.

LET GO OF OTHER PEOPLE'S PROBLEMS

For empaths, this line of negative thinking is a lot different. As mentioned, they spend a lot of time and energy trying to resolve other people's issues. You can become so focused on other people that you neglect to take care of yourself. You are always thinking about a friend or a family member's problem and punishing yourself mentally if you can't find a solution. For example, you have everything going for you, a nice home and a nice family, but your friend's car breaks down and she is extremely upset about it because she doesn't have the money to fix it. So now all you can think about is how you can help your friend raise the money to fix her car. You forget how fortunate you are to have what you have, gratitude goes out of the window and you spend your time frustrated and depressed because of a problem that doesn't even belong to you!

STOP BEING A PERFECTIONIST

Have you ever attempted to count the number of stars in the sky? If you haven't, take a shot, you will soon find out that it's impossible! Well, perfectionism is exactly the same; it is impossible to achieve. In fact, it is an unpleasant obsession that messes with your emotions, decision making, interactions, and makes overall mental clarity difficult. It is simply unrealistic to try to be perfect in an imperfect world.

For the majority of individuals, the desire to be perfect is something that was instilled in them from childhood. This might have been a parent who expected their kids to be straight "A" students or a father who put unrealistic expectations on his wife to ensure that the house was kept in immaculate condition. In general, there is nothing positive about these experiences. When the expectations were not met, there was no positive reinforcement but negative feedback, which damaged the child's self-esteem.

This type of child rearing will cause lasting damage to all children, but even more so to those who are highly sensitive. It leads to an intense self-hatred because they are unable to meet the unrealistically high expectations of their parents.

There is nothing wrong with having a desire to do things properly and wanting to be proud of your efforts. Such people are referred to as high achievers; however, many empaths suffer from perfectionism. Here are some of the character traits of a perfectionist:

Unrealistic standards: Being a high achiever is fantastic. Everyone deserves not only to want the best for themselves but to achieve it. The problem is that perfectionists tend to set unrealistic goals for themselves. High achievers set high goals for themselves, and once they have achieved them, they might have some fun and set a goal that's even higher than the last, and enjoy reaching it. Perfectionists' goals are typically so outlandish, it's virtually impossible to meet them so they become unhappy and uptight. This is one of the main reasons high achievers are not only more successful but happier than the perfectionist when it comes to goal attainment.

Procrastination: It makes no sense that a perfectionist would also be prone to procrastination. This is something you don't want to do if you want to achieve your goals. But the strange thing is that procrastination and perfectionism go hand in hand because of the fear of failure. They will spend all their time anticipating what could go wrong and what failure would look like. This leads to immobilization, and nothing ends up getting done, which leads to a feeling of failure and a vicious cycle begins.

Low self-esteem: Perfectionists are very self-critical; the slightest little thing can go wrong, and they will beat themselves up for days. They think they are not worthy of anything good happening to them. Their overall sense of personal value is already low, so when things don't go the way they had planned, they use that as an excuse to validate their feelings of low self-worth.

Push vs. pull: High achievers and perfectionists set goals for different reasons. The desire to achieve a goal pulls high achievers to accomplish theirs. Whereas the fear of not achieving pushes perfectionists towards their goals. In addition, if they do not reach their goals according to the perfect standards they have set for themselves, they view their efforts as a failure.

All or nothing: There is no such thing as "almost perfect" to a perfectionist; anything less than perfect is considered a failure to them. High achievers, on the other hand, work hard towards their goals and are satisfied even if things don't go according to plan. As long as they know they tried their best, a high achiever will always be content.

Defensiveness: Perfectionists can't take constructive criticism; they assume that they are simply being criticized and this hurts them deeply. High achievers, on the other hand, view constructive criticism as valuable information to help them improve in the future.

So, now that you have worked out that you are a perfectionist, you need to get over it because it can make life as an empath very difficult for you. Here are some tips to help you overcome perfectionism:

Get rid of whatever promotes perfectionism in your life. What are the things in your life that encourage you to be a perfectionist? Maybe you watch TV programs or read magazines that make you feel as if you are not good enough? This may not be intentional, as there is some media that contains a lot of subliminal messaging and just seeing a picture of a woman in a bikini can lead you to start subconsciously comparing yourself to an unrealistic ideal. It might even be the books you are reading or the podcasts you are listening to. Take an inventory of everything you watch, listen to and read and evaluate whether any of these media outlets could be harming you.

Evaluate your friendships. Are your friends high achievers or are they perfectionists like you? If you have more friends that exhibit the same traits as you, you may need to stop spending so much time with them. The people you associate with on a regular basis have a huge influence on you. You need to surround yourself with people who are not going to encourage or justify your behavior but with those who are not going to tolerate it and will tell you when you are saying or doing things that will not benefit you.

Become your own ideal. We live in a world with unrealistic expectations. Everywhere you look there is an image of the ideal man, the ideal woman, the ideal relationship…and the list goes on. If you have lived in this world long enough, you will know that there is no such thing as perfection—it just doesn't exist. There is nothing wrong with wanting the best out of life and working hard to make sure that your goals and your dreams are fulfilled. However, there is something wrong with continuously comparing yourself to the world's unrealistic standards. This leads to feeling that you are not good enough and that, no matter how hard you try, you will never be good enough because there is always a new ideal that you have to aspire to. The best way to handle this is to become your own ideal! In other words, become the best version of yourself, and compete with yourself to become better and better. You can do this by learning new skills to get a job promotion or a new job, going to the gym and improving your physique, or changing your wardrobe every few months. Whatever it is you feel you need to do to improve yourself, go ahead and do it. Once you have done this for a while, you can give yourself yearly evaluations:

- Look at how much you have improved in different areas of your life from the beginning of the year until now.
- Look at the things you have overcome.
- Appreciate yourself and keep your focus on your goals instead of on what other people around you are doing.

Realize that you are hurting yourself and others. Perfectionists not only place unrealistic expectations on themselves, they place them on others as well. So, you are not only hurting yourself, but you are hurting other people as well. There is absolutely nothing healthy about expecting other people to meet your standards. By doing so, you are asking them not to be themselves, but to be who you want them to be. If you are frustrated in any of your relationships, whether it's an intimate one, a friendship, or a family relationship then you might need to think about what you are expecting from them.

Understand that you are only human. Empaths have a tendency to forget that they are human. One of the reasons for this is that their gift is basically a superhuman one. The majority of people are not capable of doing what an empath can do, so your gift sets you apart from ordinary people. The thing you have to remember is that most people are reasonably balanced, as in they accept that people have flaws and make mistakes, so they are not going to judge you if something goes wrong. Unfortunately, there are going to be times when you fall short of your best. But instead of beating yourself up about it, learn to accept that it's good enough. If you know that you have put your best efforts forward, be happy with what you have accomplished and keep it moving.

LEARNING TO FORGIVE

Whether it's a simple disagreement with your partner or a long-held grudge against an old friend, unresolved conflict can cause more damage than you realize. Forgiveness is huge when it comes to controlling your emotions—think about it for a minute. If the person who has offended you invokes certain feelings whenever you think about them or see something that reminds you of them, you are going to be on a constant emotional roller coaster. Not only is this bad for your mental well-being, but it is also bad for your physical health. Some people actually think that it makes them feel good to hold bitter feelings towards someone, but scientific studies have proved otherwise.

Karen Swartz, M.D., the director of the Mood Disorder clinic at John Hopkins Hospital claims that remaining in a continuous state of anger puts the body into fight or flight mode. This results in changes in blood pressure, heart rate, and immune response. These changes then increase the risk of diabetes, heart disease, depression, and other conditions. Forgiveness reduces stress levels, which improves health.

Is Forgiveness Possible?

Yes, it certainly is, people have done so successfully in the past and they continue to do so today. There is more to forgiveness than saying you forgive someone. You have to make a conscious decision to release negative feelings towards them, regardless of what the person has done to you. Your decision to forgive is not based on whether the perpetrator is truly sorry, or whether they have suffered enough for what they have done. It is an active process on your part. When you let go of hostility, resentment, and anger, you become emotionally available to experience feelings of compassion, empathy, and even affection for the offending party.

Research has found that some people are naturally forgiving, and such people tend to be more satisfied with their lives and experience less hostility, anger, stress, anxiety, and depression. People who hold grudges are more likely to suffer from post-traumatic stress disorder and severe depression, as well as other health conditions. But this doesn't exempt them from training themselves to become more forgiving. According to a survey conducted by the Fetzer Institute, a non-profit organization, 62 percent of adults state that they want to be able to forgive more freely.

How to Incorporate Forgiveness into Your Daily Life

The act of forgiveness doesn't come naturally to most people. It is a choice that you have to make and stick to. You are choosing to extend empathy and compassion to the person who has hurt you. Here are some strategies that will help you to exercise more forgiveness in your life and improve your physical and emotional health.

Understand forgiveness: Forgiveness is an act of kindness. The person who you have chosen to forgive doesn't deserve it, but it's not about them, it's about you. This is not about excusing the behavior of the offending person or living in denial that the incident happened. Forgiveness is about freeing yourself from any negative emotions that you might have towards the individual.

Practice forgiveness: As stated, forgiveness doesn't come naturally to the majority of people—it is something that you are going to have to practice. Forgiveness is progressive; it takes time to develop. Just as you are not going to wake up tomorrow with a six pack because you did 100 sit-ups the night before, you are not going to wake up tomorrow with a heart bursting with forgiveness because you have read this book. You have to incorporate regular "workouts" into your daily routine to experience the benefits.

You can start by making a commitment to live in peace and harmony, which can be achieved by choosing not to engage in negative conversation about the person who has hurt you. You don't need to give them compliments, but if you can avoid saying bad things about them, it will help forgiveness grow within your heart.

You can also get into the habit of changing the way you view people in general. Start seeing each individual as unique, irreplaceable, and special. You can practice this ideology through a humanist philosophy or through your religious beliefs. Cultivating a mindset of placing a high value on human life will make it difficult for you to discount the person who has harmed you.

You can act in a loving way throughout your day, whether it's giving a compliment to a cashier or helping a person with their groceries. By showing love when you don't have to, you invite more love into your life, which in turn makes it easier for you to be compassionate towards people, even if they have hurt you. Turning the other cheek, so to speak, when someone aggravates you during the day can also help you become more forgiving. So instead of giving the finger to the person who cuts you off in traffic, maybe you could smile at them. Or if your partner says something that you don't like, give them a hug instead of firing back.

Remember and reflect: Think about what you have experienced, how the person hurt you, and how it made you feel. You should also think about how you felt before the incident and how you feel now. In what ways has being angry affected you?

Emotional pain comes in many different forms, including low self-esteem, self-loathing, lack of trust, unhealthy anger, depression, and anxiety. It is important to recognize and understand what you have been subjected to because of another individual so that you can work through it. Forgiveness is essential if you want to heal emotionally. Depending on the extent of the emotional pain you are experiencing, you can either come to this conclusion by yourself, or you can get professional help. However you choose to evaluate your pain, make sure it is done in an environment where you feel safe, secure, and supported.

> *Empathize with the person:* If you were or are in an abusive relationship and your partner was raised in a violent household, there is a chance that they may develop abusive habits. I am in no way telling you to remain in an abusive relationship—please get out as quickly as possible! But once you come to this conclusion, you will gain some insight into their psychological suffering and start to see them as a wounded person. Once you gain an understanding of the hurt they are carrying that led them to this point, it will be easier for you to forgive them because, despite what they have done to hurt you, they did not deserve the abuse they had to endure either.

> *Find purpose in your pain:* No one deserves to suffer, and no one wants to suffer in life, but it happens. One of the most effective ways to deal with pain is to find meaning within it. This is difficult to do because most people are

not going to want to find anything positive about the hurt they have endured. However, if you can change your perspective about it, you will reap the rewards. Has it made you a stronger person? Is it easier to empathize with others because you have experienced the same pain? When you can find meaning in your suffering, it helps you find a sense of purpose so now you can say, "Ok, you may have put me through hell, but now I am a better person because of it."

Finding purpose in your pain doesn't mean that you diminish what has happened to you. Take the time to address how you have been hurt and recognize the injustice of your suffering, but don't get stuck there.

CHAPTER 7:

LEARNING HOW TO SET BOUNDARIES

Empaths find it difficult to set boundaries because they don't like to upset, hurt, or offend anyone. In a sense, they are people pleasers, they feel guilty when they say "no," and often burn themselves out trying to help others. Empaths don't like to experience negative feelings. They feel other people's feelings, so when they are not able to help or meet someone else's needs, they feel the same pain as that person, which is what empaths find difficult to deal with.

You spend a great deal of energy worrying about situations. Even if you have a desire to set boundaries, you quickly back out because of guilty feelings. To the empath, saying no feels like a dagger through the heart because they feel responsible for that person's emotional well-being, and so you spend the majority of your life trying to avoid this.

You have perfected this avoidance technique, but the truth is that you are doing more harm than good. When you don't set boundaries from the onset, you allow other people's negative circumstances into your life, which will ultimately lead to your downfall. Before we get into how to set boundaries, let's take a look at what they actually entail.

WHAT ARE BOUNDARIES?

A boundary is the invisible line that separates two people. Boundaries put distance between your needs, feelings, and responsibilities and the responsibilities of others. The boundaries you set tell people what behavior you find acceptable and unacceptable, and how you will allow them to treat you. People who don't set boundaries are often taken advantage of. They are what I have termed "yes, yes people," your wish is their command, they can never say no.

Another way to look at a boundary is like a fence between two neighbors. Here is an example to give you a better understanding: Jason finds his neighbor irritating. She thought she was doing him a favor by taking his newspaper from his driveway and placing it on his doorstep. It was a nice gesture, and he probably wouldn't have minded so much if she didn't pick his flowers as she made her way. Jason was not at all happy about this, but he didn't want to make a fuss, so he left it alone. This went on for a few months, then her dog would find his way into Jason's garden and would poop on the grass and scare the birds away from his bird feeder. Jason continued to suffer in silence because he didn't want to cause any conflict.

The final straw for Jason came when he returned home from work to find his neighbor's children playing in his yard. They were treading on his flowers, yelling, leaving toys and trash on the ground like they were in their own home. At this point, Jason became extremely angry. Jason had no one to blame but himself. He may have felt that he was being nice by choosing to turn a blind eye to his neighbor's transgressions, but in the process, he was getting angry and irritated causing unnecessary harm to his emotional well-being.

Jason didn't set any boundaries, which made him responsible for the way his neighbor was treating him, even though she didn't think there was anything wrong with her behavior. He let his neighbor take advantage of him. What she did and what she allowed her dog and her kids to do was definitely out of line, anyone could see that. However, to start with, you could put her behavior in the gray area, acceptable to some and not to others. She didn't know that Jason didn't like her picking his flowers because he didn't tell her. The bottom line is that when you don't let people know what is acceptable and what isn't, they will undoubtedly jump to the conclusion that you are fine with their behavior.

It would have made life easier from the beginning if Jason had said, "Hi neighbor, I really do appreciate you bringing my newspaper to the door, but I would prefer to get it myself. Also, I don't really like people picking flowers out of my garden." There is nothing rude or confrontational about this statement; it draws a line in the sand that says, "This is how far you can come, but no further." Once this is made clear, whomever you are dealing with will stay on the other side of the line.

There is no point in having boundaries if they are not enforced. You have to let people know that there will be consequences if they don't respect the boundaries that you have set in place. If they are broken, go ahead and dish out the consequences. Some people have no problems accepting boundaries, whereas others will challenge you to see if you are serious. So, after Jason had set boundaries for his neighbor and she continued to break them, he would have to confront her again, and the consequences would depend on the history and the nature of the relationship.

Jason could build a 20-foot wall around his house, and unless his neighbor was prepared to fly a helicopter into his yard, there would be no way for her to get in. The problem with a 20-foot wall is that it would also keep the people Jason wants to see away, like friends and family. Basically, all boundaries should be flexible. They keep the people you don't want out but still allow the people you do want in.

WHY DO EMPATHS NEED BOUNDARIES?

Like Jason, without boundaries, you are going to have dogs pooping all over your lawn. As an empath, you have probably already experienced this with certain people in your life. You know, the ones who just take advantage at every opportunity.

BOUNDARIES PROTECT YOU

One of the many advantages of being an empath is that you have the ability to feel other people's emotions. So, you know when negative energy is about to invade your space. When you set boundaries, you keep out the energy vampires who are constantly draining you of your time and emotions.

BOUNDARIES SHOW YOU VALUE YOURSELF

"Yes, yes people" are very insecure, whether this is conscious or unconscious behavior, they are constantly seeking validation from others, which is one of the reasons they find it so difficult to say no. Empaths often believe they are responsible for how other people feel because they can pick up on it so easily. The truth is, you are only responsible for how you feel, and when you set emotional boundaries, it shows that you are not willing to allow people to take advantage of you.

Boundaries also keep you from burning yourself out—you can't take part in everything. There are going to be social events, committee meetings, and projects that you are going to have to say no to. Your priorities should come first and not everybody else's.

BOUNDARIES ALLOW YOU TO BE TRUE TO YOURSELF

People who don't set boundaries constantly have people in their space even if they don't want them there. When you don't have time to yourself, you can't be yourself because you are either trying to impress someone or cater to their needs, which is not a good place to be. You need to spend time alone so that you can make your own decisions, process your own feelings, and get your needs met.

WHY DO YOU FIND IT DIFFICULT TO SET BOUNDARIES?

We touched on this slightly earlier, but there are some deep-rooted issues that you may not be aware of that prevent you from setting boundaries in your life.

Low self-esteem: Even though you have all these magnificent powers, empaths are often very insecure. Not only do they have to deal with a weird gift that they feel no one understands, but it also leads them to seek approval from others. Empaths want to feel normal. They don't like feeling like a freak of nature, and acceptance from others gives them that feeling. So, empaths have a tendency to put others before themselves. This might sound like a selfless Gandhi-type altruistic act, but when you are doing it for approval, it becomes a problem.

Fear: Setting boundaries is not normal to empaths, as they are constantly allowing people to overstep the mark because they don't like upsetting people. Not only are they afraid of absorbing the other person's negative energy when they say no, empaths are also afraid of the rejection that may come with turning people down.

You don't know how to set boundaries: Some people simply don't know how to set boundaries. You may have grown up in a household where boundaries were not set, and so it has become the norm for you. The good news is that you can learn how to set boundaries, and I will show you how to in this chapter.

People pleasing: Empaths don't like conflict, and they would rather say yes to something than upset someone by saying no, even if it is going to be of great inconvenience to them.

OVERCOMING THE FEAR OF CREATING BOUNDARIES

YOU NEED BOUNDARIES! Especially if you are going to survive as an effective empath. And you are going to have to get used to setting them. As I'm sure you already know, people are attracted to your energy and want to be around you constantly, so you are going to have to get used to setting boundaries. Here are some tips to help you overcome this fear:

It's a healthy form of self-love. Everyone has needs and that includes you. Sometimes, you just need space to take care of you, and there is nothing wrong with that. Ask yourself this, do you feel guilty about eating more fruits or vegetables? You are probably staring at the page right now thinking, "What a dumb question!" Well, in the same way eating more fruits and vegetables is good for the body, so is setting boundaries good for your emotional health. If you wouldn't feel guilty for eating a healthy diet, why should you feel guilty about setting boundaries?

Get to know yourself. If you don't spend any time alone, you will never truly know who you are. It's practically impossible to set boundaries if you are so consumed with what everyone else needs that you don't know what you need. Spend time tuning into your feelings and thoughts. Take time out throughout the day to ask yourself, "What do I need?" and "How do I feel?" When you have a better understanding of your wants and needs, you will find it easier to set boundaries.

You are not a therapist. And even if you were, the friends who call you every second of the day are not paying for your services. It may be that with all the problems they seem to have, they might actually need some professional help.

Setting boundaries benefits everyone. Setting boundaries doesn't just benefit you, it's also good for everyone around you. When everyone understands where they stand in the relationship, it makes life a whole lot easier. Have you ever just snapped at someone for no apparent reason? Most people are going to answer yes to this question because one of the consequences of not setting boundaries is never saying how you really feel. So even though what people are doing and saying is getting on your nerves, you keep tight-lipped about it because you don't want to offend anyone. We all have a breaking point, and eventually things just get to be too much, and we end up saying or doing something we regret, and its often over something minor. When this happens, people feel as if they have to tiptoe around you in case you snap again. When you set boundaries and learn how to keep people at a distance, you will have more patience and energy.

You won't feel so much resentment and you will be less reactive.

Practice. As you know, practice makes perfect. The more you practice setting boundaries, the better you will get at it. So, keep practicing!

HOW TO SET BOUNDARIES

As you have read, one of the main reasons empaths don't set boundaries is because they don't know how to. The good news is that this is something you can learn. Here are some tips to get you started.

Take time out. The first thing you need to do is take some time out to reflect on your relationships. Get a pen and paper and write down exactly how you feel about each person and why you think they are taking up too much space in your life. Work out whether certain behaviors are the rule and not the exception. When you approach the person, you want to make sure you are not jumping to unnecessary conclusions so that you don't end up offending them.

You can't change people. As much as we would like to mold and shape people into who and what we want them to be, this is not possible. We can only change ourselves, so there is no point in getting stressed and upset about the things we have no control over. Some of the people in your life are just not going to get it. Even though you create boundaries, they will continue to push them. I am an advocate of the three strikes and you're out concept. If you have to tell someone three times that they are offending you, and they continue to violate you, cut them out of your life. It might sound a bit harsh, but their behavior is evidence that they have little respect for you. Once they realize that you are serious about your boundaries, it might motivate them to change.

What are the consequences? Before you approach anyone, you will have to decide what the consequences of breaking your boundaries will be. For example, if your partner knows that you expect them to be faithful in the relationship, but they go out and cheat, end the relationship. If you tell a friend that you are not available to talk during a certain time frame, but they call you anyway, don't answer the phone. Do you get the point? When boundaries are broken, you must enforce the consequences.

Use the correct language. When you have finally plucked up the courage to speak to this person, make sure you use the right language. People are sensitive, and the wrong words can sometimes have the opposite effect. Use phrases such as, "I want to talk to you about how I'm feeling," or "We need to work something else out because this isn't convenient for me," or "I want to let you know how I feel about…"

Don't get confrontational. In general, empaths don't like conflict; however, as mentioned above, language and the way you approach the situation is important. Stay away from sending your friend a formal invite to a "Boundaries Talk." Using words such as "We need to talk" is immediately going to put people on the defensive. Alternatively, you can use the language suggested above in the right context. Wait until the offensive behavior shows up again such as calling you at 2 in the morning or having you wait two hours while she gets ready. It is at this point that you can share your feelings and lay out your expectations about what you are willing to accept.

Don't compromise. When it comes to setting boundaries, the worst thing you can do is compromise. There should be no, "Ok, I'll do it this time." When you allow people to break your boundaries once or twice, they will continue to do so. When you say one thing but do another, people start to question your character. Once this happens, it will be very difficult for you to establish boundaries because people won't take you seriously.

CHAPTER 8:

HOW TO BECOME AN EXTROVERTED EMPATH

E mpaths are typically introverts, they have a unique way of interacting with the world. They don't really like to socialize, and they refuse to engage in small talk. An introverted empath is never the center of attention; they are quiet at social events and often leave early instead of socializing with people they don't feel comfortable with. If they do go out, they will drive themselves or find their own way there to avoid having to be dependent on anyone to get home.

In contrast, extroverted empaths are more sociable. They are talkative and don't get overstimulated and exhausted when amongst large groups of people. There is nothing wrong with being an introvert, but in general, extroverts are preferred. Those who are lively and outgoing are more exciting to be around and are often labeled as "the life and soul of the party."

Studies have found that dopamine levels determine whether a person is an introvert or an extrovert. Dopamine is a neurotransmitter responsible for several functions in the body, and one of those functions is mood regulation and has therefore been dubbed as the "feel good hormone." Research shows that introverts don't need as much dopamine as extroverts to feel good, which is why they feel comfortable spending time alone, meditating and reading, and they do not need the external stimulation from large social gatherings and parties. Extroverts get their dopamine fix from lively events and prefer to socialize in this way.

There are many reasons an introverted empath would want to become more of an extrovert.

Extroverts are rewarded. As previously stated, people prefer extroverts, which is made evident in the fact that our current culture grants more economic and social benefits to people who are outgoing and bold. The majority of famous people are extroverts; they are gifted and talented and love to be in the limelight. Even if an introvert has the gift of entertainment, they shy away from it because they don't like being in crowds.

Extroverts are happier. According to personality research, extroverts are happier than introverts, there are several reasons for this. One study found that extroverts find love easier so they are happier. Extroverts laugh a lot, which increases their levels of joy.

Extroverts are more confident. To be the life and soul of a party, you need a certain level of confidence, and extroverts have this. They don't care what anyone thinks about them.

What is an extrovert? The assumption is that an extrovert is an outgoing socialite who enjoys being in the limelight. This is true; however, there is much more to being an extrovert. If you want to become one, you are going to need a better understanding of their character traits.

They enjoy social contact. Extroverts need to be around people because this is when they are at their happiest. Socializing is a way of recharging their batteries, and they feel down and depleted when they are alone.

They enjoy novelty, risk, and adventure. Extroverts live life on the edge, and they get bored easily. They are always looking for the next thrill, making them quick to jump into new experiences and activities.

They enjoy working in groups. Extroverts enjoy working in groups. They feel comfortable when they are surrounded by people.

They like attention. Deep down everyone likes attention, but extroverts like it more than most, and will often go out of their way to get it.

The good news is that you can learn to become more extroverted if you want to. You don't have to be a shy introvert forever. Here are some tips to help you build confidence and transition from being a shy empath to an outgoing and sociable empath.

Get out of your comfort zone. In the field of psychology, stepping outside of your comfort zone is also referred to as "the optimal anxiety zone." The theory behind this concept is that when you are slightly anxious, your productivity levels increase. For example, some people do exceptionally well when they start a new job. Because they are not entirely comfortable, they go above and beyond the call of duty to prove that they can do the job.

It can be difficult to find your zone of optimal anxiety. You will need to monitor yourself constantly to discover at which point your anxiety becomes so overwhelming that it hinders your productivity.

An example of your anxiety hindering your productivity is starting a new job without the necessary qualifications or training to do the job effectively. In this instance, you are going to be extremely anxious because you know that you are not qualified for the job, which will have a negative effect on your productivity.

Push yourself. This is similar to number two but slightly different. Pushing yourself means learning and accomplishing things that you are not otherwise comfortable with, or that you didn't think you would be capable of achieving. You need to get comfortable with being uncomfortable. This will help you to embrace extroverted traits such as enjoying adventure and novelty.

However, it is important that you don't go over the top with this because you don't want to scare yourself and quit. Stepping too far outside of your comfort zone can make you anxious, so take it one step at a time. For example, if you like sitting in and watching a movie by yourself, why not invite a friend around instead? The next time invite two friends, and then you can make a trip to the movies. Can you see the progression here?

Challenge yourself. Make challenging yourself a routine in your life. It will teach you to step outside of your comfort zone and find your optimal anxiety level. As your brain becomes accustomed to trying new things, you will become less uncomfortable and begin to embrace the challenges that you set for yourself.

Be spontaneous. Extroverts love adventure and new experiences, but this is not the case for introverts. Before taking action, introverts prefer to think through and plan out every last detail. Again, start small and build up to become more and more spontaneous. For example, you can ask a co-worker that you never really associate with to go to lunch. Or if you are in a relationship, take your partner on a date without planning what you intend to do. As you practice this, you will soon start to get more comfortable with spontaneity.

Plan your group interactions. One of the reasons introverts don't like being in groups is that they get nervous about what to say and how to act. When you know you are going to a social event, plan your interactions beforehand. For example, think about different topics of conversation. Ask open-ended questions such as, "Tell me about what you do for a living." Or if you know that the person you are talking to lives locally, ask them about fun things to do in the area. People like talking about themselves, and open-ended questions are an invitation to make conversation. If you are feeling brave enough, you can also memorize some jokes to tell.

Find new ways to socialize. To make new friends, you are going to have to find new ways to do so. You don't have to go to bars or nightclubs if that is not your preference. Since I am assuming you have an idea of the type of people you would like as friends, you will need to socialize in places where you will encounter them.

Have a meet and greet. Have a small gathering at your house and ask each friend to invite a friend that you haven't met before. In this way, you will be in a comfortable environment with people that you already know introducing you to new people.

Get online. The internet is a great way to meet new people. There are plenty of social networking sites you can join to do this. Once you feel comfortable enough, you can arrange to meet up with some of your new friends offline.

Join a gym class. Gym classes are a bit more intimate than just going to the gym. The classes are small, which will make it easier for you to meet new people.

CHAPTER 9:

HOW TO BLOCK OTHER PEOPLE'S ENERGY

Empaths are blessed with the ability to absorb other people's energy. This means that they can easily detect how people are feeling. When they walk into a room, they can feel the energy of the environment. This is great when you are absorbing positive energy, but when it is negative, it can be very draining. In a sense, empaths are controlled by other people's emotions. When they are around happy people, they are happy, when they are around sad people, they are sad, and when they are around angry people, they are angry. This rollercoaster of emotions wreaks havoc on your mental stability.

When you speak to negative people, you are left feeling depleted and they are left feeling vibrant and lively because you have absorbed their energy and they have absorbed yours. Being alone allows you to feel balanced because you are dealing with your own feelings and not everyone else's. This is one of the main reasons empaths are so unsociable. Taking on other people's problems can become a burden.

Empaths are prone to addiction because they find it difficult not to absorb other people's energy. But when they are drunk or high, they relinquish their ability to feel, which provides false protection because they are damaging themselves physically. Empaths must protect their divine gift by learning how to balance and ground themselves.

Once you become more stable, you can consciously protect your energy, and you can walk into a crowded room without absorbing negative energy. If you have the gift of healing, this will also enable you to heal more people because you won't take on their sickness.

It is essential that you protect yourself as an empath; if not, life will become very difficult. Your sensitive nature can lead you to destroy important relationships and isolate you from friends and family. You need to get into the habit of grounding and balancing yourself daily so that you don't leave yourself open and vulnerable.

TECHNIQUES TO PROTECT YOURSELF

Journaling: Journaling enables you to release stuck energy and connect with your core. Energy is felt in the form of emotions, so when you write down how you are feeling, there will be a change in the energy field surrounding you.

For example, you can write down how you are feeling, and then write down how you would prefer to feel. This process will help you shift your emotions.

Detach yourself: Nothing has the power to affect you unless you allow it to. Therefore, the best way to protect yourself is to avoid getting into situations that you know will drain your energy. Empaths are constantly trying to help people because they feel their pain and sympathize with them. An energy tunnel is created any time you take on someone else's problems.

It is very endearing that you are sensitive to other people's feelings and you want to help them. However, you are not a superhero and you can't rescue everyone. In fact, some people need to go through what they are going through to teach them some important life lessons.

It will take a while for you to detach yourself from other people's emotions because you don't want to cause any offense. But once you learn to do this, you can protect yourself from unwanted negative energy.

Meditation: Meditation is a way to center and connect with yourself. It helps release negative energy and gives you balance. It is not an easy practice; emptying your mind can be very challenging, but once you get it right, meditation will be of great benefit to you. There are different techniques, including mindfulness, concentration, cultivation of compassion, tai chi, walking, and qigong meditation.

Research has discovered that meditation has several health benefits, including:

- Reduced blood pressure
- Less stress
- Reduced blood cortisol levels
- Deeper relaxation
- Increased feelings of well-being
- Less anxiety
- Improved blood circulation
- Reduced heart rate
- Slower respiratory rate
- Less perspiration

These health benefits are great, but in Buddhist philosophy, meditation frees the mind from circumstances that it can't control, such as strong internal emotions. The enlightened or liberated practitioner is no longer bound to experiences or desires, but instead has a sense of inner harmony and keeps a calm mind.

Meditation for Beginners

1. Lie or sit in a comfortable position, you might even want to buy a meditation cushion or chair.
2. Close your eyes. If you are lying down, use a restorative eye pillow or a cooling eye mask for additional comfort.
3. Breathe naturally without making an effort to control how you are breathing.

4. Pay attention to your breathing and how your body moves when you inhale and exhale. Pay attention to your stomach, rib cage, shoulders, and chest. Focus on your breath without controlling its intensity or pace. If your mind starts to drift, bring your attention back to your breath.

5. Meditate like this for two to three minutes, and then increase the time once you become better at it.

Universal vacuum cleaner: You can use this method anywhere at any time. You can even do it when you are having a conversation with someone.

1. Close your eyes.
2. Focus on your energy field to locate stuck energy.
3. Think about a large universal vacuum cleaner sucking the negative energy out of your aura.
4. Fill the empty holes by imagining white light entering your body.

Return to sender: Because empaths absorb other people's energy, the majority of your thoughts and emotions don't belong to you. You don't need to know who it came from to send it back. Simply command it to go to the center of the earth and ask your energy to transform it into light.

Spend time alone: One of the main reasons empaths like spending time alone is to avoid negative energy, but this shouldn't be your only reason. Alone time is a way to re-center and balance yourself and let go of everything that doesn't belong to you.

Spend your alone time filling yourself up with positive energy by reading inspirational books, listening to motivational speakers, meditating, or any other activity that you find rejuvenates and refreshes you.

CHAPTER 10:

HOW TO COPE WITH A FLOOD OF EMOTIONS AT ONE TIME

Have you ever experienced being in a crowded place and it feels like you know what everyone in the room is thinking and feeling? It is so intense that you feel like you are no longer in your own body? Unless you learn how to feel balanced at all times, being an empath can feel like a curse instead of the blessing that it really is. Here are some tips to help you deal with feeling so many emotions at one time.

> *Take care of yourself:* This might sound cliché, but you will be shocked at the number of empaths who don't take care of themselves and then complain that they can't handle the influx of emotions they have to deal with. Your mind, body, and spirit are connected, and they should all be in alignment with one another.

Eating junk food is going to make you feel sluggish, lazy, and irritable. The better you eat, the more powerful your physical body will become. You will have a clear mind and it will be easier to listen to your inner voice. It is also important to exercise. Moving the body helps to release blockage and build-up from the negative energy you have absorbed from other people.

Everyone is different, and you will need to find what suits you best. Eat organic food because it doesn't contain any preservatives. I am in no way saying that you should become a vegan overnight, but consume more plant-based foods than animal products, eat less sugar and processed foods. If you are going to eat meat, make sure it is grass fed, and limit your intake of dairy products (You can read more about this in chapter 14).

Balance and moderation are key. You should never feel as if you are depriving yourself, and you shouldn't become so obsessed with it that you become stressed and anxious. Taking care of yourself should be fun and enjoyable, and it will become even more so when you start seeing results.

Visualization and aura cleansing: I don't have enough space to go into detail about this, but what I can tell you is that it works. To get a better understanding and some guided instructions, go to YouTube and type in "Empath Meditation" and "Aura Cleansing Meditation." There are some really good videos to get you started with this, but here are some basic steps to cleanse your aura.

- Set a timer for five minutes and find a comfortable place to sit down and relax.

- Imagine that a cleansing white light is beaming all over you.
- Imagine that the light is healing you and getting rid of anything that is not benefiting you.
- Make a conscious decision to release anything that doesn't belong to you such as emotions, feelings, thoughts, and experiences.

Cleanse your life: What makes you miserable? Is it something that you can stop doing? What leaves you empty and exhausted? Who makes you feel like this? As you become aware of your abilities as an empath, you will notice that you attract people who drain you emotionally—they are called "energy vampires." Where are you going on a regular basis that drains you, where people are constantly taking from you, but you are not getting anything back? Identify these people and places and eradicate them from your life.

Eliminate things that don't agree with your spirit: Anything that doesn't benefit you, things that you are doing just to please others, has to go. If you are invited to an event or a friend asks you to do something that your spirit doesn't agree with, say no! You are going to feel bad when you turn down invitations because you don't like disappointing people, but the truth is that if your spirit is automatically telling you no, it means that something isn't quite right, and you probably won't enjoy yourself anyway. Think back to how many times you have ignored your instincts, and you arrived at your destination, got bombarded with negative energy, and got home feeling mentally exhausted? You have probably experienced this more times than you care to admit. By getting rid of the things in your life that don't agree with your spirit, you are protecting yourself from having to deal with a multitude of negative emotions that you would rather not experience.

Protection Meditation – The Jaguar Method

There are certain powers you can call upon to give you extra protection when you are in need. Empaths often use this method when they are overwhelmed with negative energy. First, let's talk about why the jaguar is so important.

Who is the Jaguar?

A jaguar is a wild cat species native to North America. It is the third largest cat in the world and the largest cat in the Americas. It is a very powerful animal and kills its prey with one deadly bite to the skull. Like empaths, they prefer to spend time alone, and they only socialize with females for mating purposes.

Jaguar Symbolism

The jaguar is viewed as a symbol of strength and life, as well as several other meanings:

- Rejuvenation
- Beauty

- Loyalty
- Courage
- Spiritual power
- Valor
- Fertility

The Black Jaguar Spirit

The black jaguar spirit is beautiful and graceful; the animal is relentless and fast when it comes to pursuing something that it wants. These are the same qualities the jaguar wants you to have when it comes to fulfilling your dreams and desires in life.

It is also a symbol of the power of silence. It hunts and stalks its prey silently and then pounces when it is least expecting it to. Therefore, as an empath, it is important to know when to make your presence known and when to stay in the background.

The jaguar also represents your strong ability to tune into the vibrations present in the atmosphere. When you are interacting with people, the spirit expects you to be in control of your emotions as well as hear the unspoken words of those you are communicating with. The black jaguar is also a symbol of the secret gifts you should be sharing with the world, which includes your knowledge, strength, grace, power, and beauty.

It is also a symbol of your speed and agility in terms of how you handle certain issues in life. It has a strong ability to understand chaos and help you move through the trials and tribulations that you go through in life.

The black jaguar can stare without blinking, he has big mysterious eyes that can see right through to your soul and discern your innermost thoughts and feelings. It symbolizes how you can reclaim your true power and it teaches you how to trust your instincts.

How to Call Upon the Black Jaguar Spirit With Meditation

When you are in a situation that requires additional protection, I recommend calling on the power of the jaguar for assistance. Use it when you are being bombarded with negativity and feel as if things are getting out of control.

- Get into a calm meditative state by taking long and slow deep breaths.
- Feel the presence of the jaguar as it enters into your space.
- Imagine this powerful, beautiful creature slowly walking around your energy field and creating a barrier so that nothing negative can get in.
- Visualize what the jaguar looks like—its deep black fur, piercing golden eyes, statuesque body, and the elegant intentional way in which it moves.
- Feel secure as the jaguar encircles you.
- Thank the jaguar and know that you can call upon him whenever he is required.

CHAPTER 11:

HOW TO FIND PEACE LIVING IN A CRUEL WORLD

There is no denying the fact that we live in a vicious and evil world. You just need to turn on the television, flip through your local newspaper, or turn on the radio to hear the atrocities that are continuously taking place around us. We are constantly bombarded with images of war, murder, and hatred, and it can become extremely depressing if you focus on it. I can't tell you why the owners of the media are so hell-bent on barraging us with negative content, but I can tell you that there are also plenty of good things happening in the world.

12-YEAR-OLD BOY FEEDS THOUSANDS OF HOMELESS PEOPLE

Massachusetts is a better place because of a 12-year-old boy named Liam Hannon, the pioneer of "Liam's Lunches of Love." In his free time, he travels around the city of Cambridge providing lunch for the homeless. He has given out more than 2,000 lunches in bags that he writes handwritten messages of encouragement on. Liam believes that he is spreading a message of joy and hope to the less fortunate, and he hopes that it will ignite something in them to achieve a better life.

Liam's father, Scott raised $44,000 through a GoFundMe page to buy a food truck so that Liam can expand his operation and travel across Boston to give out free lunches.

450 STUDENTS SERENADE DYING TEACHER

After being diagnosed with cancer, more than 450 students from the Christ Presbyterian Academy in Nashville gathered outside his home to sing Christian songs of worship. Despite his radiation and chemotherapy, Ben Ellis continued to teach his students Latin and Bible studies. This beautiful act of kindness went viral receiving 31 million views after it was posted online.

BROOKLYN BROWN'S BENEFIT PROJECT

Brooklyn Brown is a kindergartner who, as an infant, was diagnosed with juvenile rheumatoid arthritis. When she has an arthritis flare, she finds it difficult to walk, needs help going to the bathroom, and sometimes needs a wheelchair to get around. But despite her illness, Brooklyn has a big heart and puts others before herself. Knowing what it's like to spend weeks in the hospital, she decided to do something to help sick children stuck in hospital beds.

Brooklyn started raising money to buy crayons for the kids so they would have something to do when they were waiting for doctors, nurses, or visits from their family and friends.

You Become the Change You Want to See

It is a fact that the world we live in is a very evil place; unfortunately, there is nothing you can do about this. You can't control how other people choose to behave, but you can control your actions. Instead of getting depressed about the wickedness that is so prevalent today, you become the change that you want to see. Choose to radiate love every day, whether it is to friends, family, or strangers, make the decision to do something nice for someone. It doesn't have to be anything major. You could buy a homeless person lunch, buy your mom a bunch of flowers, or help an old lady across the road. The idea is to take positive action and become the best person you can be despite the fact that the world is going crazy.

Become a Volunteer

Becoming a volunteer is a great way to show kindness and give back to your community. Volunteering is perfect for empaths because they are such selfless people. Volunteering helps switch your focus and enables you to do what comes naturally to you and put others before yourself. It creates social cohesion bringing communities together, connects people, and unites people of different religions, cultures, and walks of life. If you are an empath who tends to isolate yourself, volunteering is also a way to get you to socialize more.

CHAPTER 12:

MAKING CAREER DECISIONS AS AN EMPATH

The majority of jobs involve working with people, whether directly or indirectly, so you are going to have some human contact. Therefore, empaths often find it difficult to work or find a job that is suitable for them. If you are going to excel, you will need to find work that you enjoy and that, to a certain degree, understands your sensitivities. You need to express your creativity, quietness, thoughtfulness, and intuition instead of trying to fit in and become a part of the crowd, which is what happens in most work environments.

CAREERS THAT EMPATHS THRIVE IN

In general, empaths excel when working alone, in low-stress jobs, or when working for smaller companies. They are also more comfortable working a full or part-time job from home, away from the chaos of an office environment, where they are not micromanaged nor forced to deal with frustrating office politics. They prefer to communicate over the phone, through email or text message to limit face to face interactions. Working like this enables you to plan your own schedule, set your own rules, and take breaks at will when you need to recharge your batteries.

Empaths prefer to be self-employed to avoid being overwhelmed by coworkers, managers, frequent meetings, and demanding schedules. If being self-employed is too risky for you, some businesses allow you to work from home. With advanced technology such as Skype, emails, text messages, and access to the internet, it is not always necessary to work in an office. So, you may be able to split your time during the week so that you are working from home for a few days. One important point to take into consideration is that you need to be careful not to become too isolated when working from home. Neither do you want to overwork yourself, because this is easy to do when you don't have a nine to five schedule. You should also take some time out to socialize with friends and colleagues.

If you are self-employed, you prefer working as artists, health care assistants, editors, writers, and other creative professions. Several musicians and actors, such as Jim Carey, Scarlett Johnson, Alanis Morrissette, and Clare Danes have admitted to being "highly sensitive." Other jobs you might want to consider include plumber, electrician, accountant, virtual assistant, graphic designer, website designer, real estate agent, and business consultant. These professions are fine as long as you are self-employed and can set your own schedule and establish solid boundaries with your clients.

Forest ranger work, gardening, landscape design, or other employment opportunities where you are required to make contact with the environment are also good for empaths. You might also want to consider jobs that are focused on preserving the earth and her ecosystems.

Empaths also enjoy work where they help others because of their innate desire to serve people. They find great satisfaction in this type of work as long as they don't absorb the stress of their patients and are able to take time out to nurture their own needs. Empaths often become life coaches, hospice workers, clergy, massage therapists, Chinese medical practitioners, yoga instructors, teachers, social workers, psychotherapists, physical therapists, dentists, physicians, employees of non-profit organizations or volunteers, as well as a host of other jobs that involve caring for people. Empaths are also animal lovers and find it satisfying to work with animals as dog groomers, veterinarians, or in animal rescue.

To really do well in any of the mentioned helping professions, empaths can't afford to take on the symptoms and stress of their patients. They can do this by taking regular breaks to meditate and focus on themselves. You also need to set clear boundaries and limits with your clients and take enough time outside of work to refuel and relax. On the other hand, empaths are likely to find jobs such as firefighters, doctors, nurses, and police officers too stressful. Despite the fact that they involve helping people, there is too much sensory stimulation and continuous physical and emotional turmoil for empaths to deal with.

Empaths are valuable in any profession; however, you must find a career that supports your gifts, skills, and temperament. So, when you are searching for a job, use your intuition to discern whether you are a good fit for the values of the company, the energy, the people, and their overall goals. A job might have all the right credentials on paper, but it has to sit well with your spirit.

CAREERS THAT EMPATHS SHOULD AVOID

A job that you are not suited for will drain your energy leaving you feeling weak, tired, and regretting that you are an empath. This is something that you want to avoid—you want to protect your gift, not deplete it.

One of the worst jobs for an empath is sales, which is especially true if you are an introvert. Spending too much time speaking to people and dealing with angry customers is too stressful for an empath. Also, empaths absorb people's stress and emotions, which can make them sick. One empath I know said that working as a cashier nearly gave him a panic attack—the crowds, the noise, the bright lights, and the loudspeakers were all too much for him. He had to leave in the first hour of starting his job. Whether it's advertising, selling jewelry or cars, empaths don't enjoy having to be on call all day.

Other careers for empaths to avoid include trial attorneys, executives with large teams to manage, politics, and public relations. As mentioned, empaths are typically introspective, sensitive, thoughtful, and soft-spoken. These high-stress professions value extroverts, aggressiveness, and the ability to engage in small talk.

The mainstream corporate world is also a problem for empaths because such environments have a certain code of honor. Money is their main motivation. They don't value people, and it's a dog eat dog world where individuals will do anything to get to the top. Empaths are independent thinkers and will challenge the status quo if it doesn't feel right to them. They like to understand the reasons behind why a decision has been made so that it feels right to them.

How to Handle Taking Disciplinary Action in a Leadership Role

Being an empath has its positives and negatives when it comes to being in a leadership or management role. You can tap into your employees' emotions and know when something is bothering them, which makes you very relatable. On the other hand, empaths don't like conflict and would rather avoid it if possible, which means that as a manager, there is the potential for your employees to walk all over you, which doesn't look good in the work environment. Unfortunately, there are some things that are inevitable as a leader, and one of them is taking disciplinary action against your employees. Here are some tips to do so successfully.

The best way to ensure that things go the way they are supposed to is to prepare yourself beforehand.

Review the details. This should be your first step. What is the reason for taking disciplinary action against this employee? Has there been a complaint lodged against this person? Are they not being productive on the job? Make sure you have your facts straight before you sit down and speak with the employee. If you need evidence, collect it before the meeting.

Know the HR policies and procedures. Knowing the company policies about the alleged infraction will give you the confidence you need to approach the situation in a professional manner. It means that the employee won't be able to talk their way out of the situation because you have the facts and the company's policies on hand.

Know your objective. There is no point in having a discussion with an employee if nothing is going to come out of it. Even if you are just issuing a formal warning, let the employee know that this is what you are doing, and make sure that it is logged in their file.

Be firm, empathetic but professional. Being empathetic is something that comes naturally to you, so you won't find it difficult to think about what it will be like to take their place. Even if they were at fault, the employee is still going to be nervous, upset, and scared during the disciplinary hearing. Keep this in mind while speaking to them, but also remain firm and professional so they know that the matter is serious.

Once your objective has been achieved, end the conversation. There is no need to let the meeting drag on. Have the meeting, say what needs to be said, and shut it down.

As an empath, you are going to feel upset for two reasons—it is in your nature not to want to upset anyone and you are going to feel the person's pain and want to make it right. Therefore, resist the temptation to apologize because it's not your problem. Remember, whatever rules were broken, that employee chose to break them. They have made their bed, now they have to lie in it.

Please bear in mind that if you are currently in one of the professions that empaths should avoid, I am in no way telling you to pack up and leave. That would be totally irresponsible of me. But you can find solutions to make your time at work suit your needs better. When empaths are happy, they become extremely valuable in their chosen field.

CHAPTER 13:

HOW TO DISCONNECT FROM WHAT'S GOING ON AROUND YOU

Although the majority of empaths are introverts and would rather spend their time alone than with groups of people, they are constantly a part of the mix. Not because they want to be, but because it is in their nature. Whether an empath goes to the store, a social event or they are in a lecture hall, they connect to the energy in the atmosphere, and when that energy is bad, it can have a terrible effect on them. Here are some tips on how to disconnect from what's going on around you.

REGULAR CENTERING

The most effective way to disconnect from what's going on around you is through centering. As you have read, when you are triggered into an empathetic state, your energy fields are opened, which causes you to absorb other people's energy and for you to release energy to others.

Centering allows you to take your energy back by closing those openings. It is what Eckhart Tolle refers to as "being present," using mindfulness and focus to bring yourself back into a healthy state. This is where you are completely aware of how you are feeling at that moment in time, and you are focused on yourself instead of what's going on around you. When you are centered, you are less likely to become distracted and get overwhelmed by other people's energy.

HOW TO CENTER YOURSELF

The main intention of any energy management exercise is to focus on your intention. It is the power of your intention that centers you. Were you aware that you can control your chakras through the process of visualization? In other words, your thoughts and intentions control your energy field. You make the rules and your energy responds.

Most of us do this without realizing it. Negative thinking depletes your energy, and anything you do that doesn't line up with your morals and values depletes your energy. On the other hand, when you repeat positive affirmations, comfort or empower others, your energy field expands. Your energy reacts to everything you say or do.

This is something you may know in theory, but if you are not practicing it, it won't do you any good. Controlling your energy is not an easy task. If it was, negative energy would have been eliminated from the planet a long time ago.

Regular centering helps you to maintain control of your thoughts and energy. Most importantly it is a constant reminder of what it feels like to be centered. You can then tap into this feeling at will when you get too emotional-ly attached to what's going on around you. The following steps will help you get centered.

1. *Get quiet:* Still your mind by focusing on your breath for 2 minutes.

2. *Ground yourself:* You can ground yourself through the process of visualization. Imagine the energy of your root chakra whizzing through the earth and wrapping itself around the earth's core, then com-ing back to you in the same way.

3. *Energy retrieval:* This is where you tell your energy to return to you. Thought energy can be absorbed by past events, fears, loved ones, and people around you. Wait for a few minutes and then call that thought energy back to you.

4. *Close your openings:* You are going to have some openings in your energy field at this point, so you will need to close them. You can do this by imag-ining white light burning at the heart chakra and then reaching out to close the openings. You might hear doors closing at this point.

5. *Experience your energy:* Focus on being silent within, self-aware, and present. Remain in this state for as long as you can.

6. *Remind yourself that you can do this:* Remind yourself that you can enter into this state any time you feel that your chakras are open and you are absorbing too much energy.

If you feel as if you are carrying other people's baggage, you can release this energy before you center yourself. Follow these steps to do so.

1. Shut your eyes.
2. Say out loud, "God" or "Archangel Michael."
3. Then say, "I now call on the source of power to eliminate any energy that is not mine. It is done, it is done, it is done."

Centering is something that you are going to have to practice, and the more you practice, the better you will become at it. Not only will it enhance your empathetic abilities, but you will also have more control over the energy you are absorbing, and where your energy goes.

To master the art of centering yourself the moment you need to, you will have to be very self-aware and have a deep understanding of your empathy triggers. If you don't have a high level of self-awareness, don't worry, you will learn how to raise it in the next section.

HOW TO RAISE YOUR SELF AWARENESS

Most empaths know that they are empaths, but they don't understand that there is a process to it. This is one of the main reasons empaths don't know how to disconnect. They assume it's natural to be in an empathetic state all the time.

In case you have forgotten, let's go over what happens when you tap into other people's energy.

1. Your empathy is set off by something.

2. The doors to your energy fields are opened up and you start experiencing the energy of another person or persons. This is good if you are trying to help someone because you are better able to empathize with them.

3. The doors to your energy fields should close once your job is done, and you should return to your normal self. If you are an unskilled empath and don't know how to close the doors to your energy field, they will stay open and you won't know that they are open.

So, to turn your empathy off, you must be aware of what is taking place when it is happening. This means that your self-awareness needs to be very precise. You will need to practice this regularly to become an expert at it.

To begin, you need to learn what sets off your empathy. It could be one of the following, or something completely different. When you think about it, you will know what they are.

- Violence or aggression on TV
- People suffering
- Someone who disagrees with you
- Someone who needs you for something

Who triggers your empathy the most? Is it family members and loved ones, or just people in general?

The next step is to pay attention to the empathy process. Observe what happens when you are in an empathetic state. What is your main focus at that particular moment in time and when does it happen? It could be when you are walking down the street, having a conversation with someone in a social setting, listening to a friend's problems, or observing the people around you. It is the norm for empaths to focus on other people, so there is a chance that you may not have noticed how much you do this.

When you realize that you are getting sucked into the vortex of another person's energy, it is at this point that you need to call your energy back. You can do this by pinching yourself and paying attention to the physical sensation, or you can pay attention to a color that you like, a piece of artwork, or a piece of furniture. The more you practice this, the better you will become at it, and it will develop into a habit that helps you subdue your empathy.

You can also call your energy back to you and command the doors to your energy fields to close at that exact moment. Take a minute to observe how you feel and what's going on in your spirit. Visualize the open doors to your energy fields slamming shut. If you can get deep into your visualization, you can also imagine the sound of the doors closing. If not, make an affirmation that it is taking place.

TRANSITIONING FROM THE CONSCIOUS TO THE UNCONSCIOUS

If you have spent time practicing the centering process and you are not getting good results, there is something blocking it from working, and you will need to find out what that is. There will be times when you are unable to turn off your empathy because a part of you wants to keep it on.

You may even experience feelings of guilt when you turn it off. Some empaths feel as if they need to remain in a constant empathetic state because without it, they won't be able to help people the way they need to. If this is how you feel, here are some steps to overcome this fear.

Your gift is a sacrifice. There is nothing fun about absorbing other people's negative energy. In some instances, this is required. If you are constantly taking the world on your shoulders, it will eventually damage you and you won't be any good to anyone.

Empathy should be switched off. Simply put, it is unhealthy to remain in a constant state of empathy. How will you ever get to know yourself if you are continuously submerged in other people's energy? You need alone time.

Minimize co-dependency. Empaths are often co-dependent because they can become so attached to someone else's pain that they almost feel as if it's their pain. You will do everything in your power to help the person out of their situation, not only because you don't want them to suffer, but because you don't want to feel their pain anymore. When boundaries are merged like this, the situation can become very tricky, which is especially true if the other person is also an empath.

CHAPTER 14:

HOW DIET PLAYS A ROLE IN ENERGY

Empaths who understand the importance of diet consume a vegetarian or plant-based diet, and this is not purely for ethical reasons. When your digestive system is at peak performance, it uses a lot of energy. Meat, in particular red meat, is very difficult to digest. According to the Mayo Clinic, meat and fish can take as long as two full days to fully digest. This is because the fats and proteins they contain are sophisticated molecules that the body finds difficult to break down. By contrast, foods that are high in fiber such as fruits and vegetables take less than 24 hours to digest. They move through the system easily because their natural substances help the digestive system to operate more effectively. This means that after you take your last bite of Popeye's chicken, the body spends much of your precious energy trying to digest it.

Empaths need all the energy they can get since they are constantly being depleted of it. Consuming foods that are full of nutrients and easier to digest is a simple way to give yourself that much needed additional energy boost.

I am not going to tell you what you should and should not eat. I have simply given you the information, and it's up to you what you choose to do with it. Some foods are going to agree with you and others won't, so your first step should be to determine which foods work for you and which foods don't. Most nutrition experts recommend an elimination diet, which is where you cut out certain foods one at a time to zero in on specific sensitivities. Once you have pinpointed the foods that harm, it's time to start eating the foods that heal.

I am not a dietician or an expert on foods, but once I realized that my diet played an important role in my empath capabilities, I began to research and experiment with food. I have found that the following foods work best for me.

- Fruits, especially lemons, limes, tomatoes, avocadoes, apples, mangoes, berries, and bananas
- Raw vegetables, especially celery, zucchini, and red pepper
- Cooked vegetables, especially cauliflower, brussels sprouts, broccoli, string beans, and kale
- Raw greens, especially parsley, basil, lettuce, and spinach
- Garlic smoked tofu
- Grains, especially oatmeal, gluten-free pasta, quinoa, and white rice
- Seeds and nuts, especially raw cashews, almonds, tahini, natural peanut butter, chia seeds, and ground flax seeds

- Organic sauerkraut
- Organic dark chocolate
- Vegan protein powder
- Vegan cheese
- Condiments such as hot sauce, Dijon mustard, and apple cider vinegar
- Olive oil and coconut oil
- Foods rich in vitamin B12 such as nutritional yeast and almond milk

I find the following foods problematic, so I have eliminated them from my diet.

- Red and white meat and fish
- All dairy products including eggs, yogurt, cheese, milk, and butter
- Refined sugar
- Gluten
- Caffeine
- Alcohol

As you will notice from my food list, my current diet leans more in the direction of vegetarian and plant-based. Changing my diet has resulted in better digestion, consistent blood sugar levels, high energy levels (I no longer feel the need to take a nap in the middle of the day), clear skin, reduced PMS, and improved moods. I am also more mentally focused, with an improved ability to concentrate on tasks for longer periods of time.

CHAPTER 15:

TIPS FOR RAISING AN EMPATH CHILD

E mpath children are special and unique, but to a parent who doesn't understand the gift, it doesn't come across that way. You may think your child is needy, emotional, and oversensitive. You may have even punished your son or daughter because they tend to act out in ways you don't understand. You want them to be happy but don't think that encouraging their sensitivities will help them in the long run. You may have accused your child of being too emotional (this is especially true for boys) and told them that they will need to grow a thicker skin if they are going to make it in this world.

You have been to counseling, therapy, spoken to friends and family, but you just can't seem to figure it out. The thing is that you love your child and you refuse to give up on them, so you continue seeking answers and fate has led you to this book. This chapter will help you if you are not sure whether your child is an empath, or if you know your child is an empath and want some advice on how to raise them successfully.

SIGNS THAT YOUR CHILD IS AN EMPATH

Always feeling unwell: Does your child always have an upset stomach, a headache, or a sore throat? Are they constantly complaining that they are in pain? Do you walk into grocery stores and your child is fine, then five minutes later they are complaining that something is wrong? Most parents chalk this behavior up to attention seeking, and some doctors have even labeled children as hypochondriacs. However, the reality is that highly sensitive people pick up on other people's illnesses, and they can become so in tune with the other person that they actually start feeling their pain.

Although it can get quite frustrating having a child who is always sick, you should never take it out on them. Now that you know that they are not attention seeking, showing your child that you are concerned, you care, and are there to support them is the most effective way to handle this trait.

Extremely sensitive to the emotions in their environment: Empath children will tap into every emotion that is around them. If you and your husband have had an argument and you are trying to hide your anger from the kids, your empath child will pick up on it. Emotionally, there is nothing you can hide from them. Empath children latch onto things such as energy, atmosphere, and body language.

There is no point in trying to hide your emotions from an empath child because they will pick up on them immediately. What you can do is be as open and honest with them as you possibly can. Obviously, there are some things that children don't need to know. In these circumstances, let them know that there is a problem, and you are trying to resolve it, but try not to avoid telling them because they are too young to understand. With everything else, you will make things easier for you and your child if you tell them the truth.

> *Very responsible:* While you might think that your child just enjoys being helpful, it runs a lot deeper than that. Empaths feel as if other people's happiness is their responsibility, so much so that they will abandon their own needs to go above and beyond the call of duty to help someone. If they can't, they get very upset with themselves. An empath child might take on worries and responsibilities that they are too young to handle. You may have already experienced this, but don't be surprised if you are ever struggling with the bills and your child gets upset because they are too young to go out and get a job to help.

Let your child know that you are grateful for their help but that they are too young to intervene in adult affairs and mommy and daddy have it all under control. Encourage your child to relax and have fun and continue to reinforce that it is not their responsibility to make other people happy. Once you can get your son or daughter to understand this, it will free them to enjoy their childhood without having the burden of feeling they are responsible for other people's problems.

> *Difficulty sleeping:* Are there times when your child finds it difficult to sleep at night? Empath children can become exhausted and anxious if they are overstimulated, including having too many things to do throughout the day without taking enough breaks, multi-tasking, and no alone time. They then find it difficult to wind down at night because they are still feeling the stimulation in their system from earlier in the day.

Empath parents are not the only people who struggle to get their kids into bed on time—it is a common problem. The only difference is that empath children are not being defiant when they don't want to go to bed, they simply find it difficult to go to sleep. Here are some tips to help you with this.

Establish a Night Time Routine. Children need structure; it provides them with a sense of security and safety when they know what's coming next. A bedtime routine will help your child develop sleep associations to let them know that it's time to go to bed. A good routine might include:

- Taking a bath
- Brushing their teeth
- Putting on pajamas
- Getting into bed
- Reading a story
- Goodnight hugs and kisses

You can change the routine depending on what works best for your child. It's important to remember that it's not what you do during the routine, but how consistent you are with it.

Avoid stimulating drinks. One of the main ingredients in soda is caffeine, and if you allow your child to drink a can of soda, make sure you give it to them early on in the day so that it doesn't affect their ability to sleep.

Turn off electronics. Kids love gadgets just as much and if not more so than adults. If allowed to, they will continue to play with them right up until bedtime. The light emitted from the screen emulates daylight and tricks the brain into thinking that you should be awake. All electronic devices such as games, laptops, and televisions should be switched off and locked or removed from the room an hour before bedtime.

Provide a good sleeping environment. Your child's room should be conducive to sleep. Ideally, the room should be cool, dark, and quiet. Some children don't like sleeping in the dark, so in such cases, a small lamp would be appropriate. Soft playing nighttime music will also help your child fall asleep as well as drown out any of the other sounds in the house.

They find it difficult to tolerate noise: Are you getting frustrated because your son doesn't like going to the game with you? This isn't because he doesn't like sports, but because he is unable to tolerate crowds, clapping, cheering, booing, and loud music. Basically, noise is a huge irritant to empath children.

Short of keeping your child locked up in the house, there is no way to avoid exposing your child to loud noise. There are some things you can do to reduce his or her discomfort.

Let them wear earmuffs or earplugs. Earmuffs are great for blocking out sound, and there are plenty of fun looking earmuffs and earplugs that your child will enjoy wearing. If you are going to a noisy event, take a pair with you to drown out the sound.

Encourage your child to take breaks. When taking your child to a noisy event such as a family gathering, as well as wearing earplugs, you can also take him or her outside for a break when it appears that things are getting a bit too much. This will help them settle down so they can go back and enjoy the rest of the event.

> *Disliking people or being in certain environments:* You might think that your child is rude because there are some people that they are just not able to tolerate. This may come in the form of them refusing to say hello or running from them when they come to the house. Do you dread taking your son or daughter to certain places because you know they are going to start acting up? That's because they don't like the environment because there is negative energy and bad vibes that they are unable to handle.

Empaths have very strong intuition, and they automatically know when something is not right. If they don't like one of your friends or a family member, trust their judgment and distance yourself from the person. It will probably save you from problems in the future.

If your child doesn't like being in certain environments, don't force them to go there. It will only make your kid anxious and depressed, and you wouldn't want to be responsible for upsetting them.

CHAPTER 16:

A STEP BY STEP GUIDE TO LIVING YOUR LIFE AS AN EMPOWERED EMPATH

L et's face it, living life as an empath is difficult, and there are many ways to ease any issues that may arise. If you want to embrace your gift and live life as an empowered empath, here are some suggestions you could incorporate into your daily routine.

Some of these steps have already been mentioned throughout the book, but there is no harm in being reminded of them. Remember, you are more powerful than you think, and you can tap into that power through consistent practice.

Love thy self: Yes, it might sound cliché, but before you do anything else, you need to focus on loving yourself. I want you to put your gift to the side for one moment and concentrate on loving you for you. Whether you want to accept it or not, you are a person before you are an empath and that's what you need to focus on.

Think about when you first meet someone. Unless they are an empath, they are not going to know you are an empath. Once you get to talking and they decide that they like you, they will do so because of your personality, and maybe the things that you have in common and nothing else.

Empaths can be more insecure than the average person because they are so different. This will hinder your ability to live an empowered life. So here are some tips to help you love yourself a bit more.

What have you achieved? Accomplishments are an essential part of life, but sometimes we do not give ourselves enough credit for them. Get a pen and paper, sit down in a quiet place, and write down everything you have achieved in life. There is no time limit on this exercise. If you can remember something from when you were three years old, write it down.

What do you like about yourself? Most people don't think about this because we are so focused on what other people like about us. But when you realize that there are actually things that you like about yourself, you will start loving yourself more.

Get clear on your goals. There is nothing worse than having no purpose in life. Years go by, and before you know it, ten years have passed and you haven't achieved anything. However, when you know what you want out of life, and you are intentional about getting there, you won't feel so hopeless, which will help you love yourself more.

Spend time alone. Empaths are so focused on everyone else that they forget about themselves. They are constantly basking in other people's energy, and the majority of the time that energy is negative. Take time out each day to saturate yourself in your own energy.

Eat healthy foods. Food should be a very important part of an empath's life. Food is energy, and the more junk food you eat, the more you are surrounding yourself with negative energy. Consume a plant-based diet, eat lots of fruits and vegetables, and drink a lot of water.

Use crystals. Empaths function at their best when they are surrounded by high vibrational energy. Crystals can help you achieve this. You can either wear them around your neck or carry them with you in a small bag. Some crystals are better than others—choose those that hold the highest vibrational energy, such as:

- Black tourmaline prevents negative energy from coming into your field, and it is good for grounding.
- Labradorite protects your aura and blocks negative energy from draining you.
- Rose quartz helps you to love yourself more and emit a high love frequency.

Meditate. Meditation helps you to connect with yourself. It calms the mind and the soul, allowing you to connect with your spirit guides to get the help that you need.

Set boundaries. Empaths are terrible at setting boundaries. They find it extremely difficult because not only do they feel responsible for other people's happiness, they don't like to offend people. However, it is important to set boundaries as an empath to prevent burnout.

Practice self-awareness. The more self-aware you become, the easier it will be to discern when you are tapping into someone else's energy. You all know that dreaded feeling, one minute you are fine and the next you feel anxious, worried, scared, or depressed. The good news is that it doesn't have to paralyze you. Take some time out and acknowledge the fact that these feelings don't belong to you. Do a self-check, and whatever you are feeling ask yourself if it is justified. If not, you know it has come from someone in your environment.

Invest wisely. Just as in the finance world, there are good and bad investments, and the same principle applies to your life. There is nothing wrong with extending a helping hand, but there are some people who refuse to listen, won't take your advice, and will continue to do what doesn't benefit them. You should feed such people with a long-handled spoon or they will drain your energy.

Stay away from parasites. Unfortunately, empaths attract the wrong kind of people. Because you are so kind, open, and sensitive, you attract people who will manipulate, use you, and don't have your best intentions at heart. When you meet someone for the first time and something just doesn't feel right, trust your instincts and stay as far away from that person as possible.

Establish a morning routine. And last but not least, establish a good morning routine. Consistency is the key to living as an empowered empath. You want certain behaviors to become the norm for you. The only way this will happen is if you practice them daily. Here are some ideas.

- Wake up early, ideally between 5 am and 7 am
- Meditate for 10 minutes
- Journal, write down any dreams if you had any
- Read or listen to something positive
- Focus on your goals by going over your vision board
- Say some affirmations
- Write a to-do list
- Exercise
- Have breakfast
- Shower
- Go to work

Well, that's all folks, now it's time to get to work, remember – the more you focus on these steps and put them into practice, the stronger you will become!

CONCLUSION

I have made a deep connection with my inner desire to become a blessing to the world, to push humanity to become all they were created to be. One of the reasons I wrote this book was to use my experience and abilities to help as many people as possible to live happy, fulfilled, and spectacular lives. This desire has manifested in ways that I could not have even dreamed of. When I think about everything I have accomplished in such a short amount of time, I am completely blown away.

So, let me ask you, what impact do you want to have on the world? What gifts and talents can you use to fill a void in someone's life? Please understand that when you are living your best life, you bring light to everyone who crosses your path. By embracing who you were destined to be, by living a blissful and dynamic life, you inspire the people you are surrounded by to do the same. Being your authentic self is one of the most important keys to successfully living life as an empath. I want you to be empowered, embrace your gift, and live a life that brings joy and abundance to the world!

THANKS FOR READING!

I really hope you enjoyed this book, and most of all got more value from it than you had to give.

It would mean a lot to me if you left an Amazon review – I will reply to all questions asked!

Simply find this book on Amazon, scroll to the reviews section, and click "Write a customer review".

Or alternatively, please visit www.pristinepublish.com/empoweredempathreview to leave a review.

Be sure to check out my email list, where I am constantly adding tons of value. The best way to currently get on the list is by www.pristinepublish.com/empathbonus and entering your email.

Here I'll provide actionable information that aims to improve your enjoyment of life. I'll update you on my latest books, and I'll even send free e-books that I think you'll find useful.

Kindest regards,

Judy Dyer

ALSO BY
Judy Dyer

Grasp a better understanding of your gift and how you can embrace every part of it so that your life is enriched day by day.

Visit: www.pristinepublish.com/judy

Made in the USA
Las Vegas, NV
17 September 2023